HANDWRITING WORKBOOK

FOR KIDS AGES 4-12

WORDS, PHRASES AND ALPHABET PRACTICE

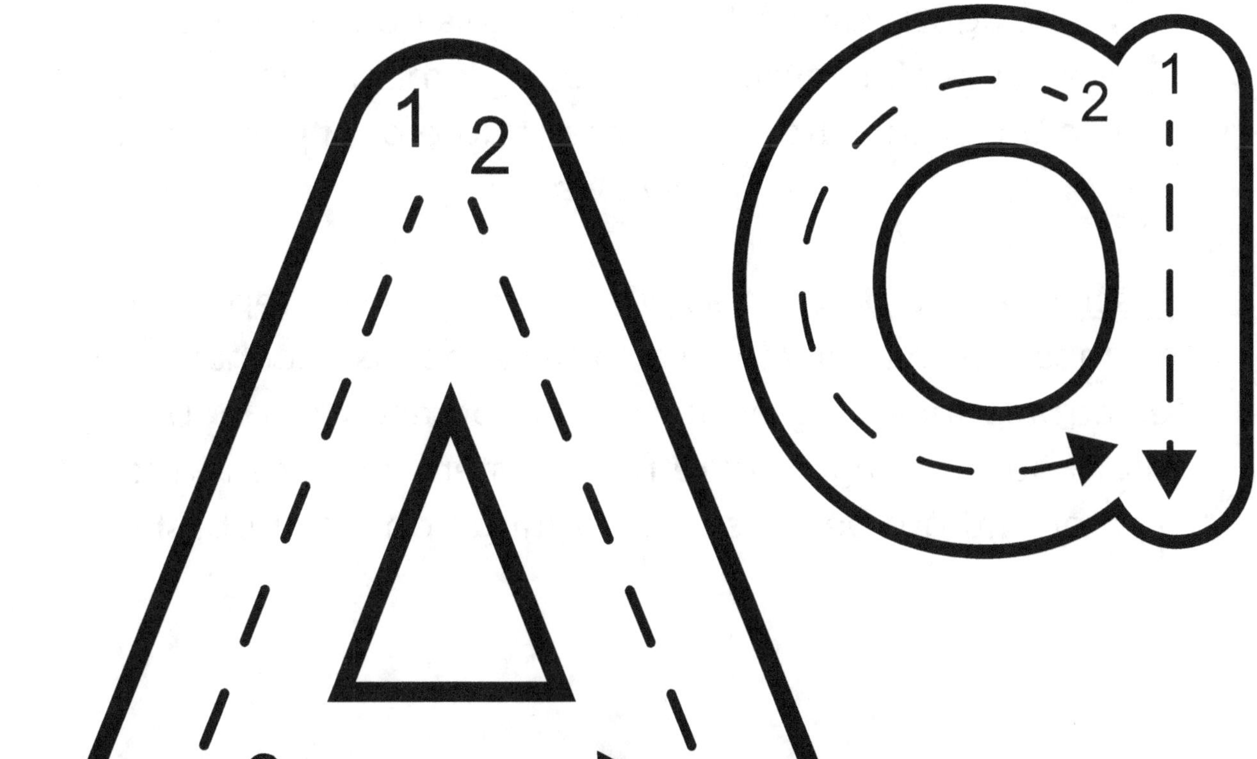

By: Emma Carter

THIS BOOK BELONGS TO

• — • — • — • — • — • — • — • — •

• — • — • — • — • — • — • — • — •

UPPERCASE HANDWRITING PRACTICE

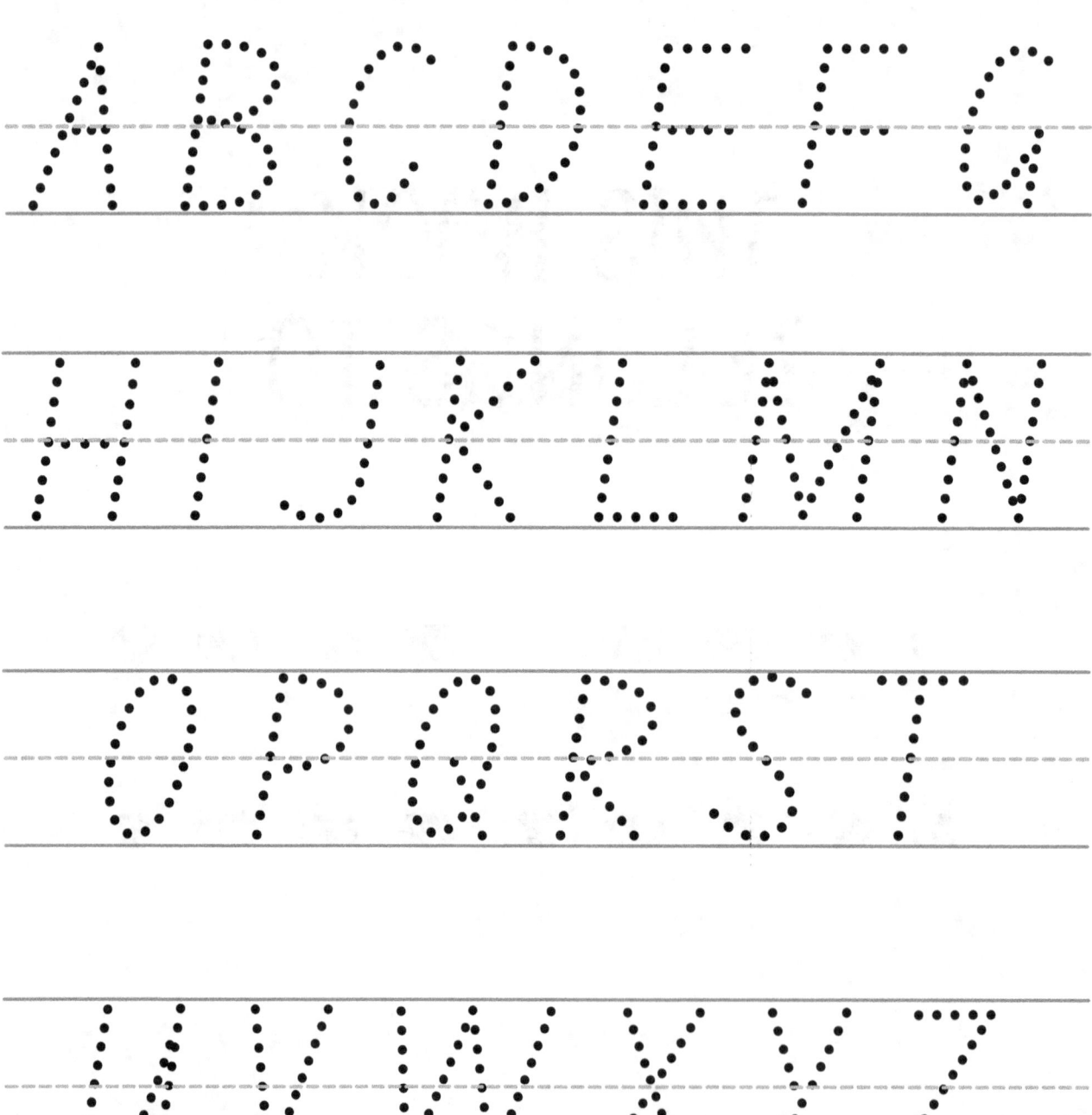

Lowercase Handwriting Practice

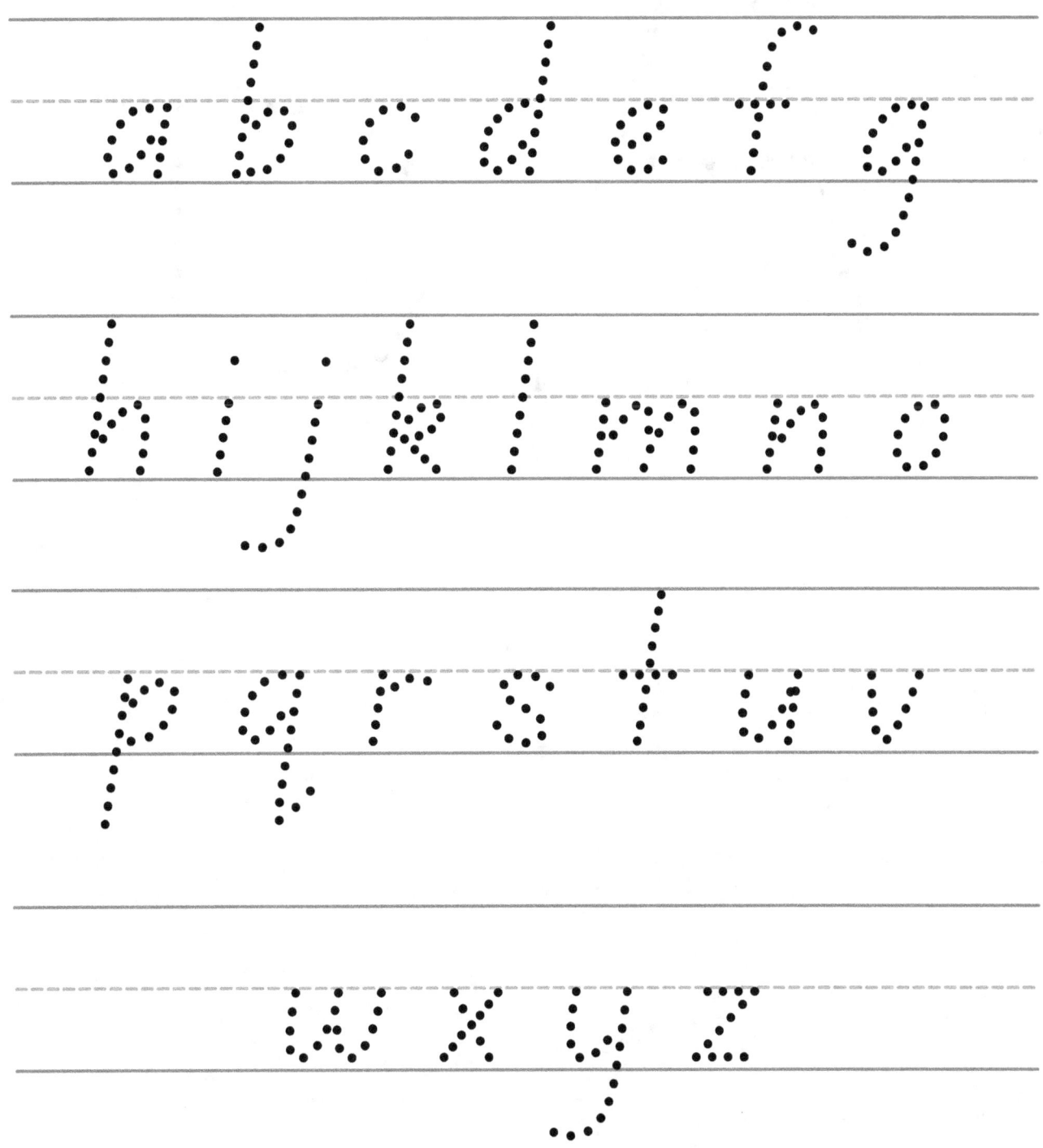

A

a

A

a

A a A a A a A a

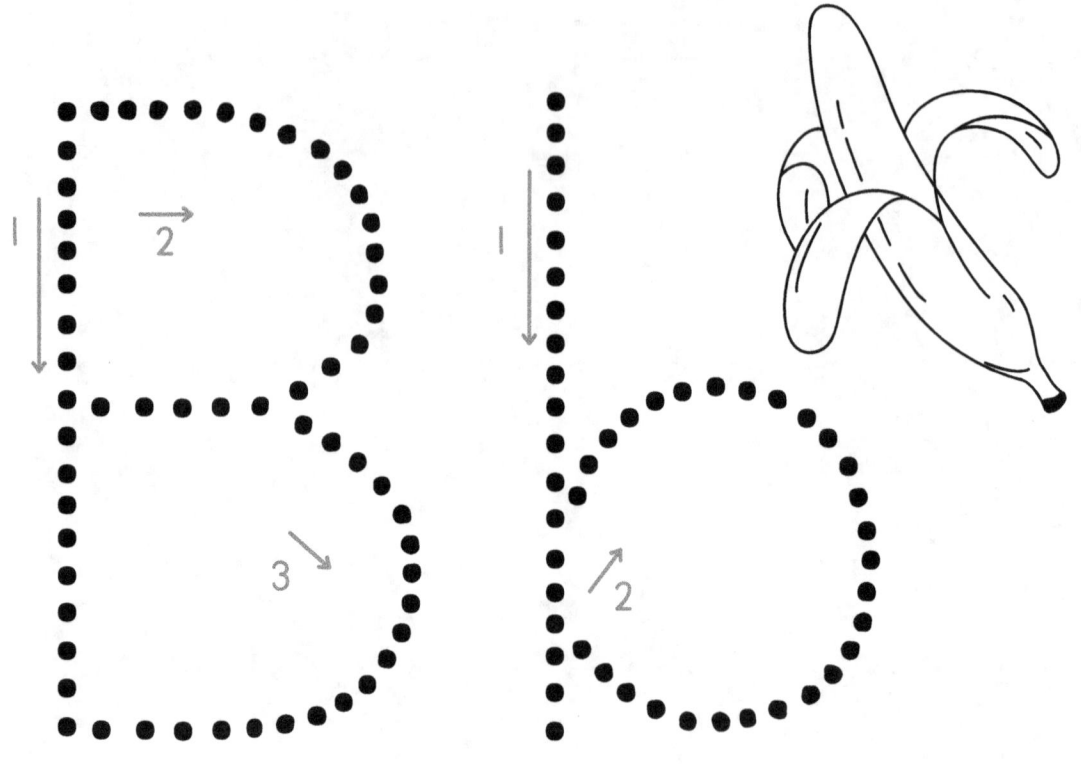

B

b

B

b

B b B b B b B b

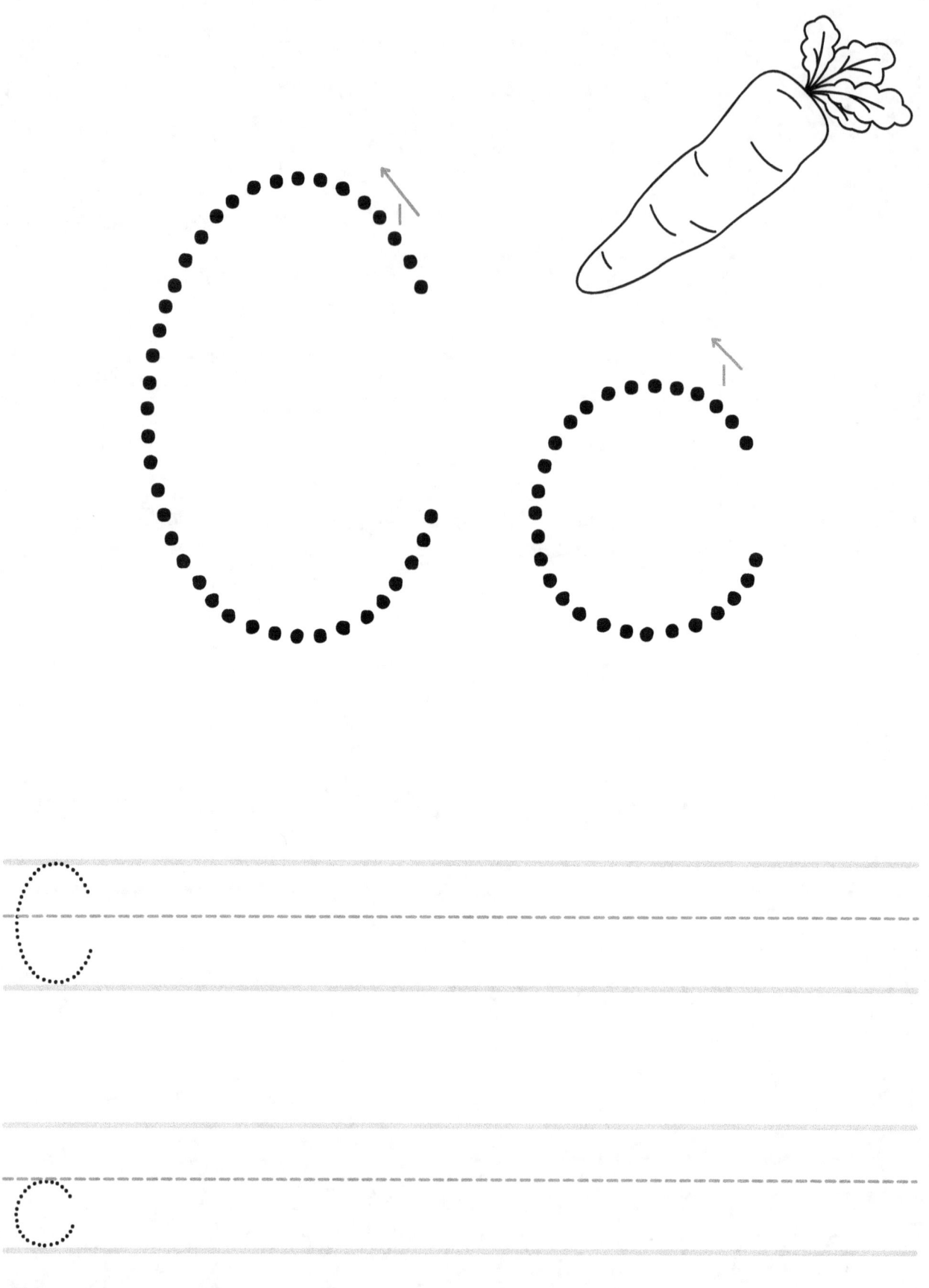

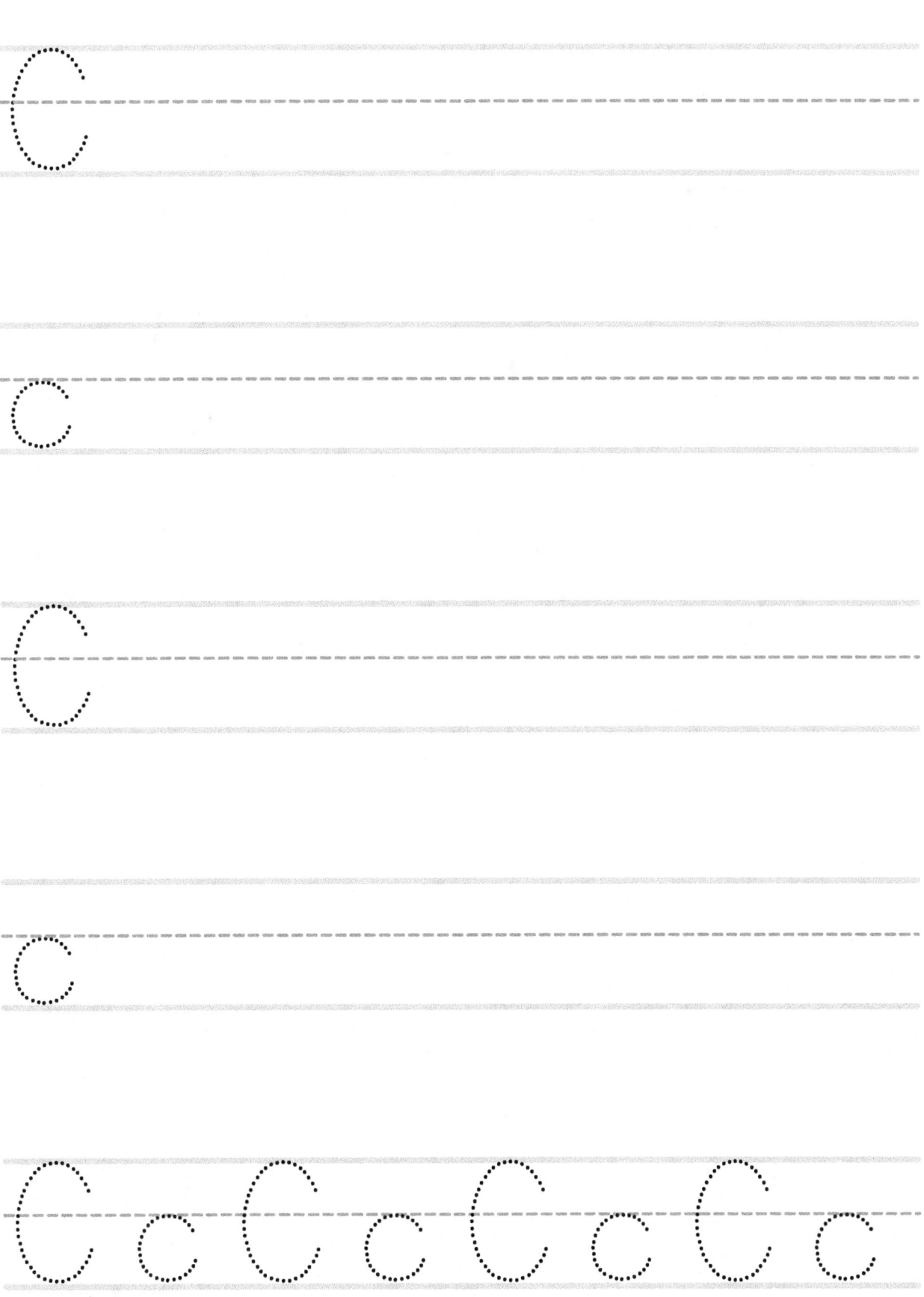

D

d

D

d

D d D d D d D d

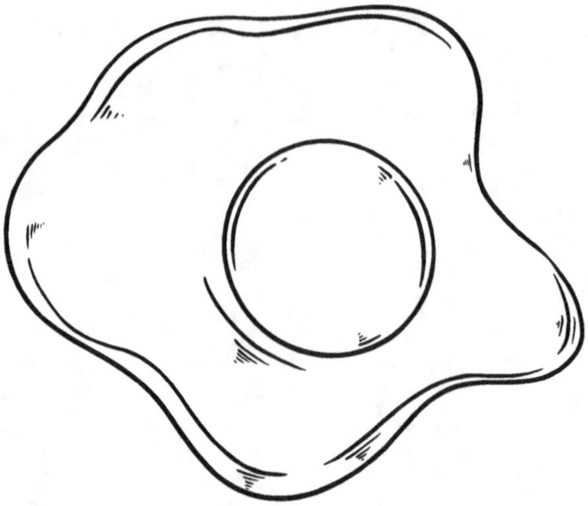

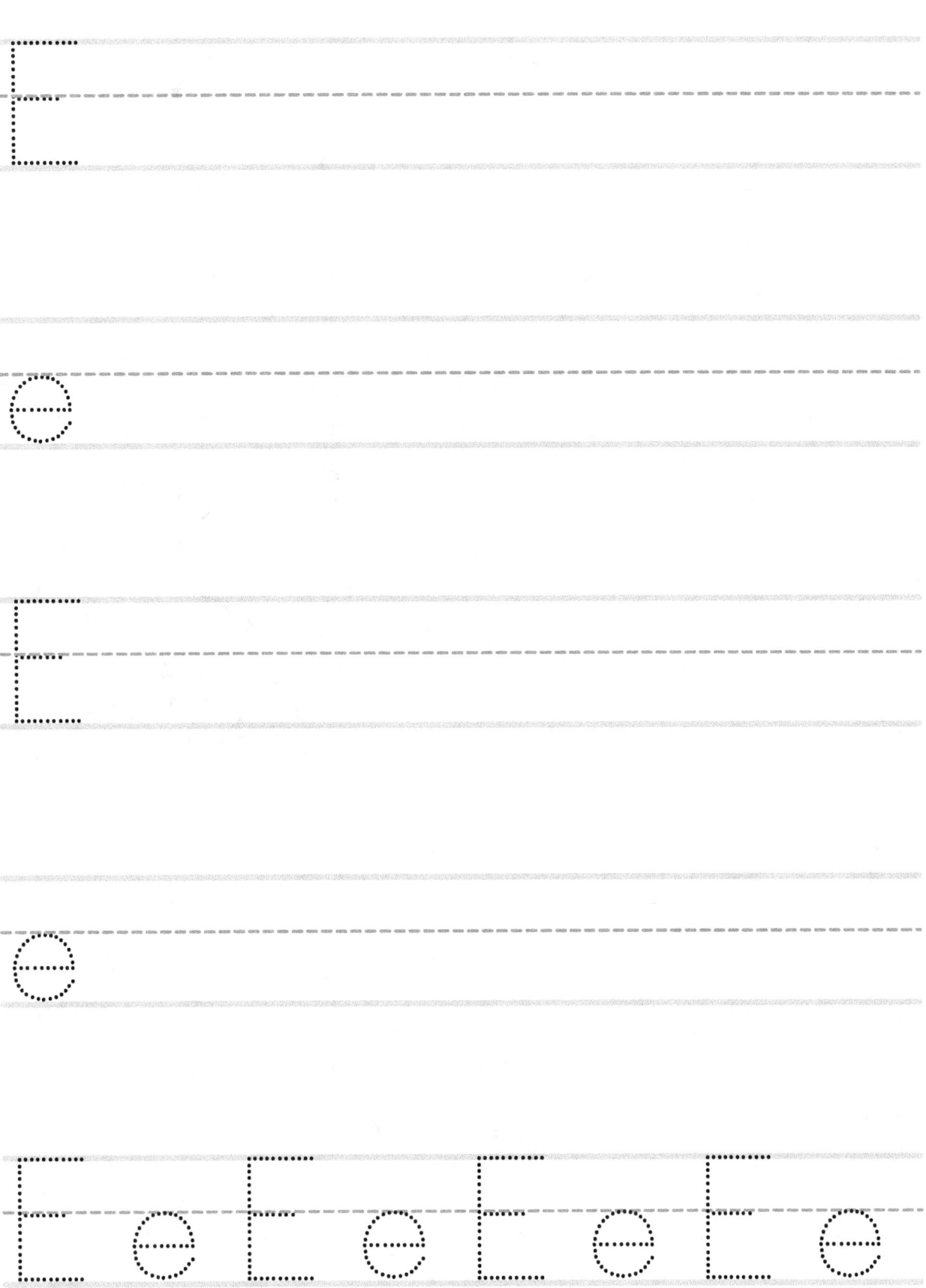

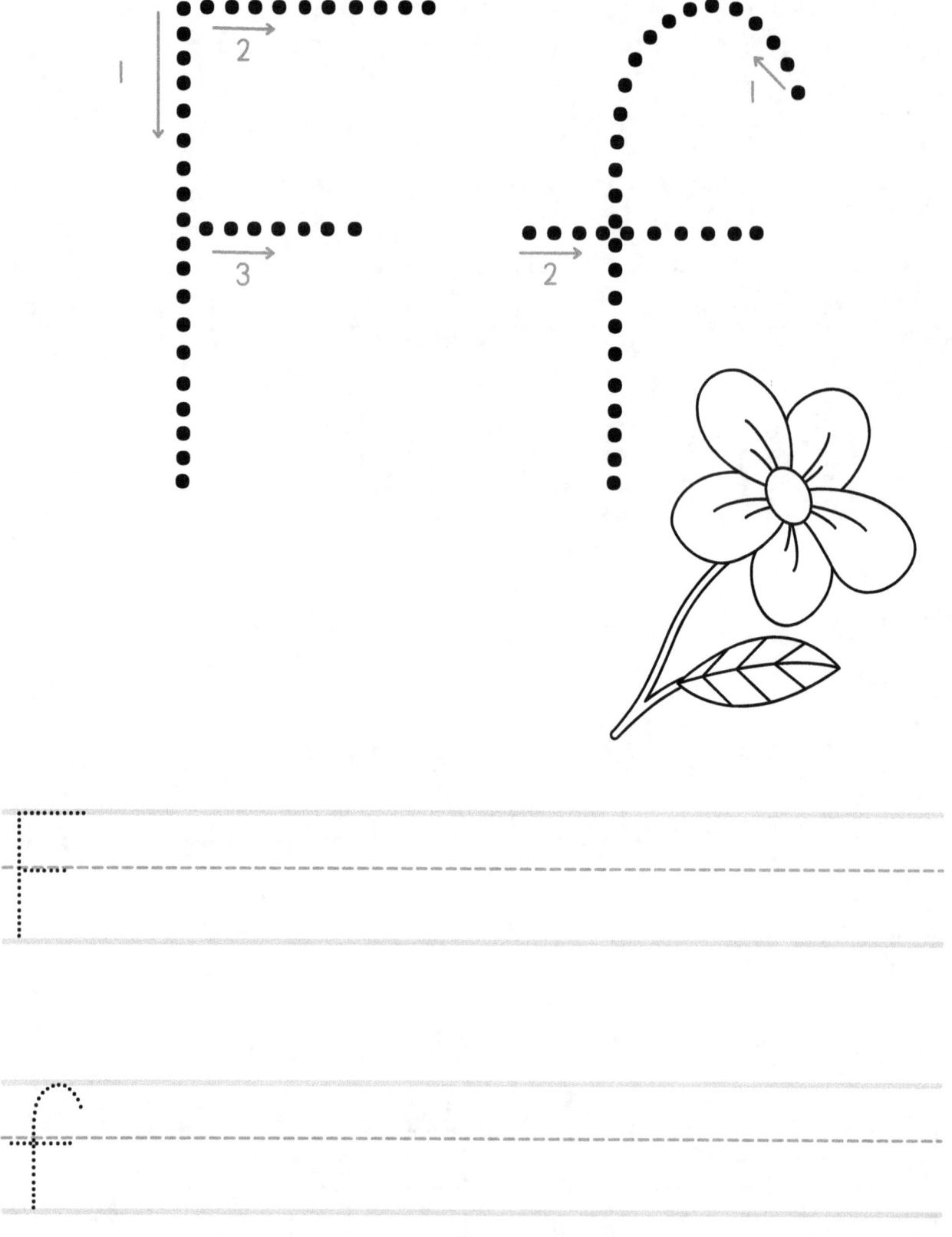

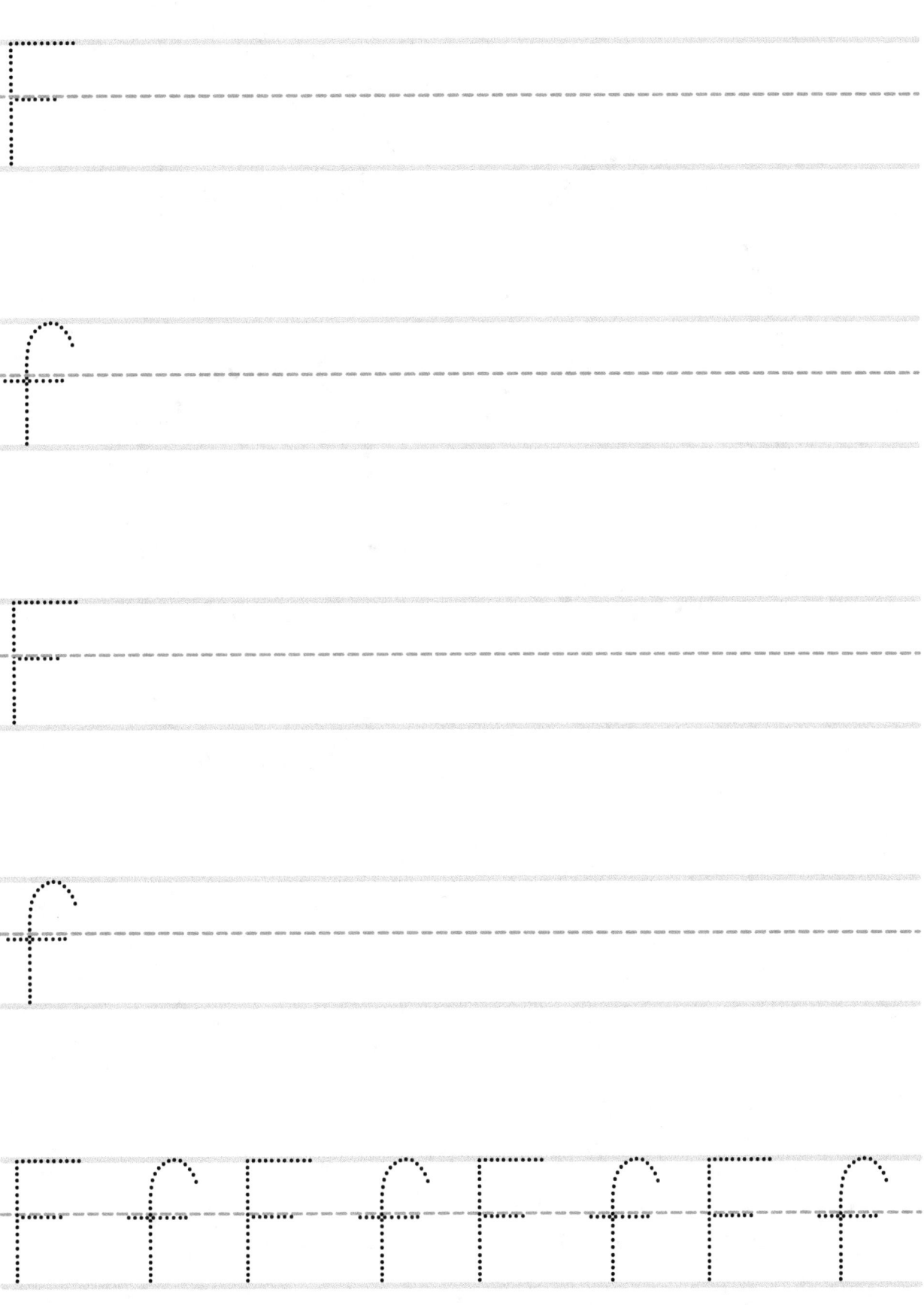

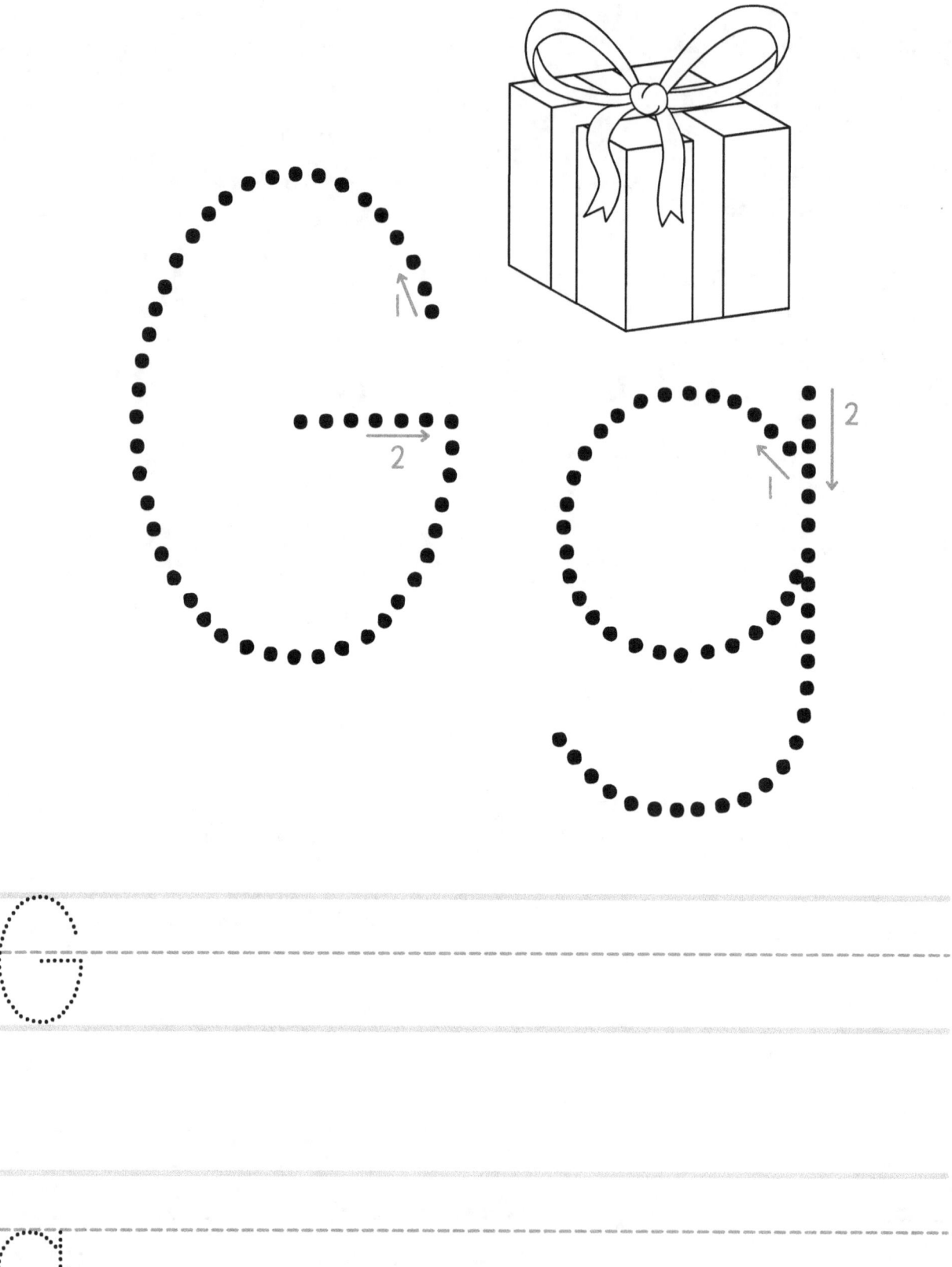

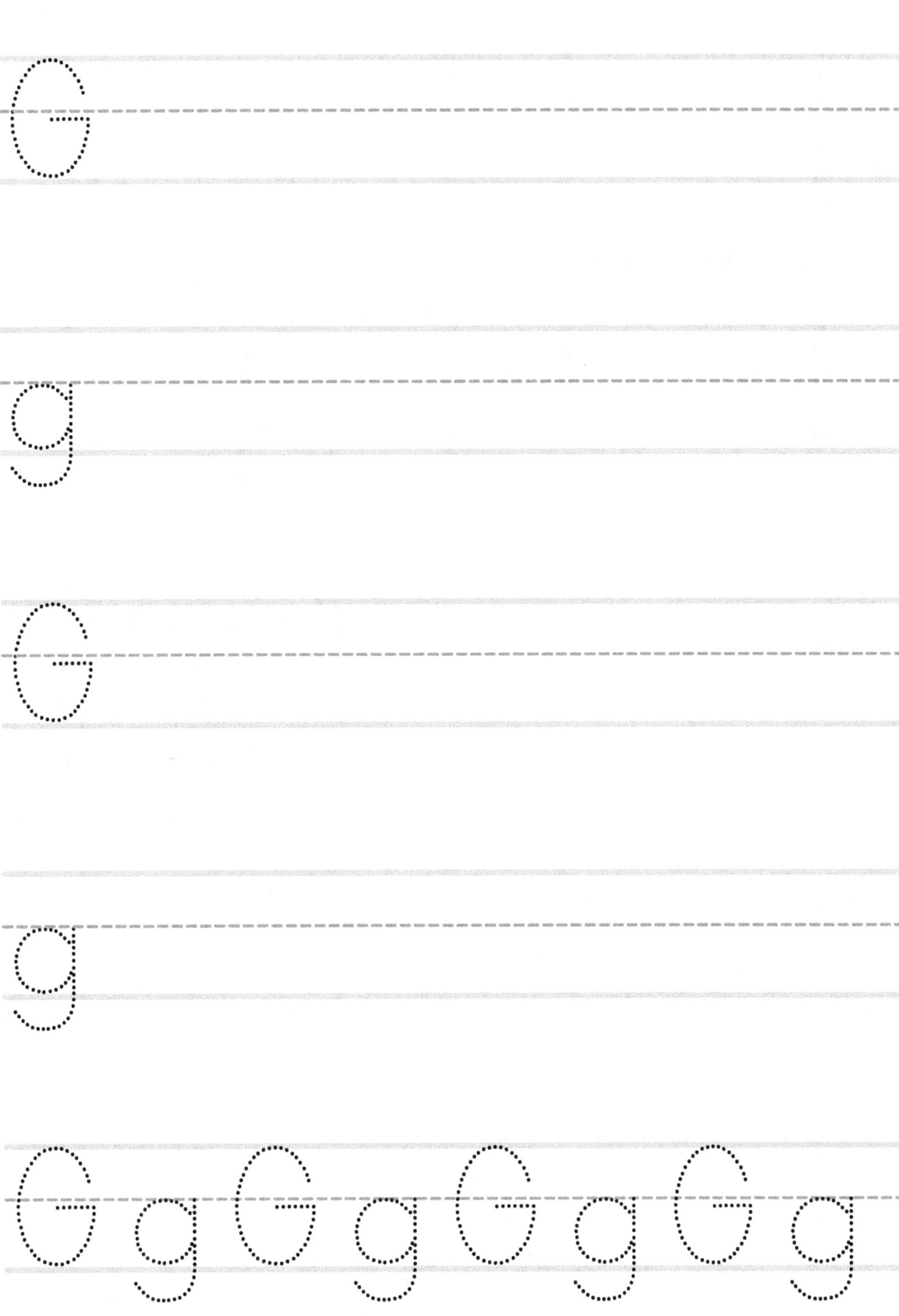

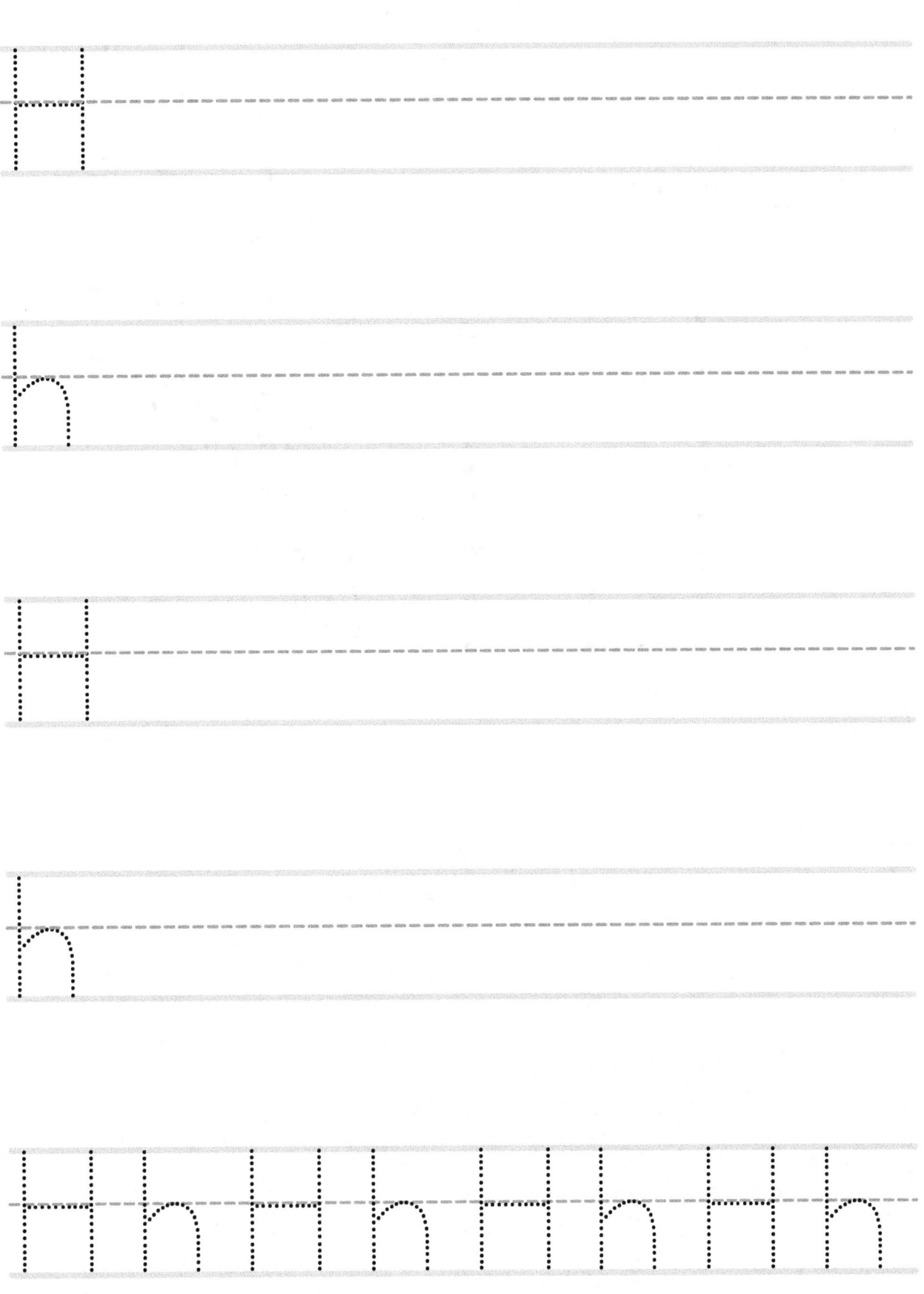

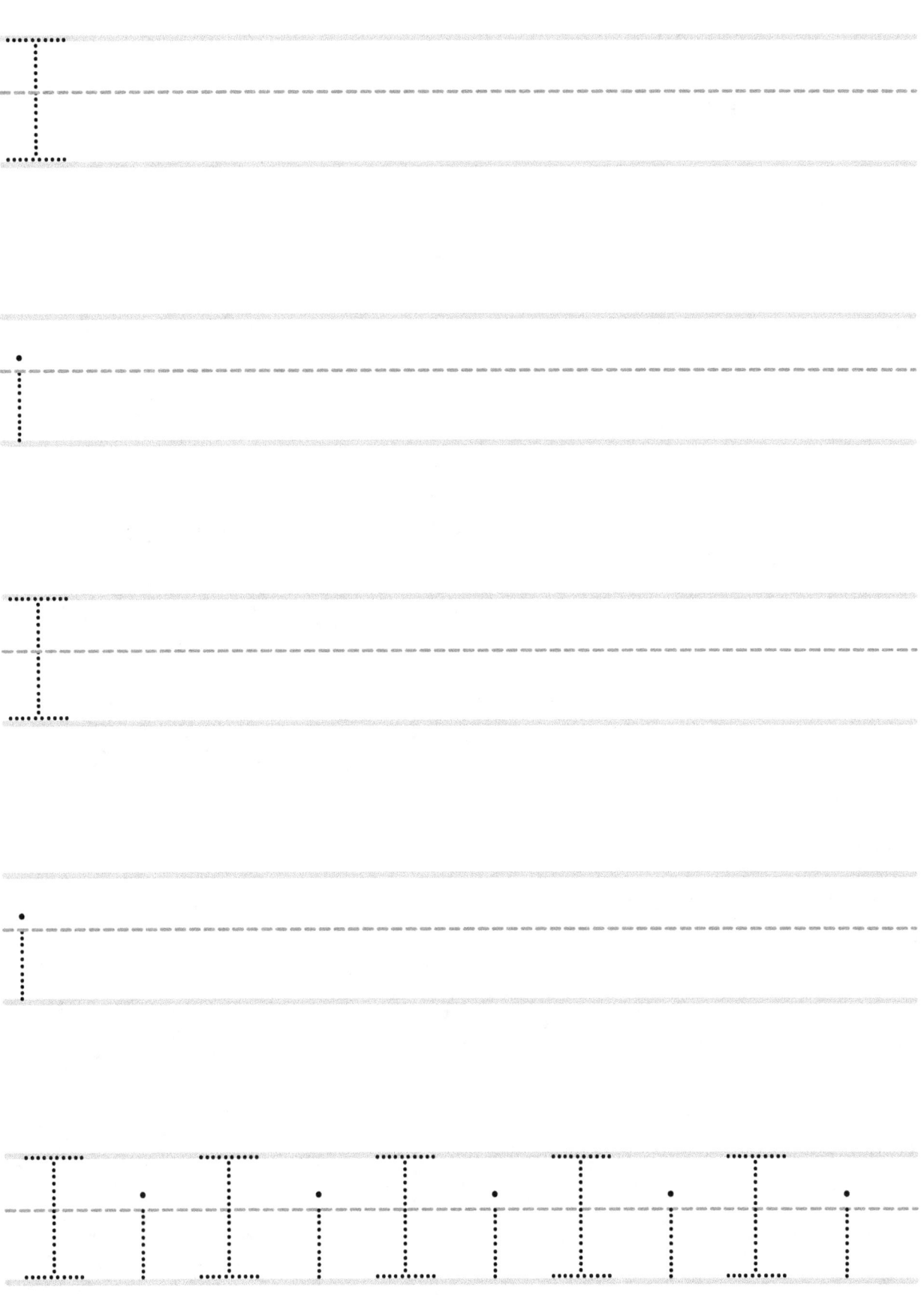

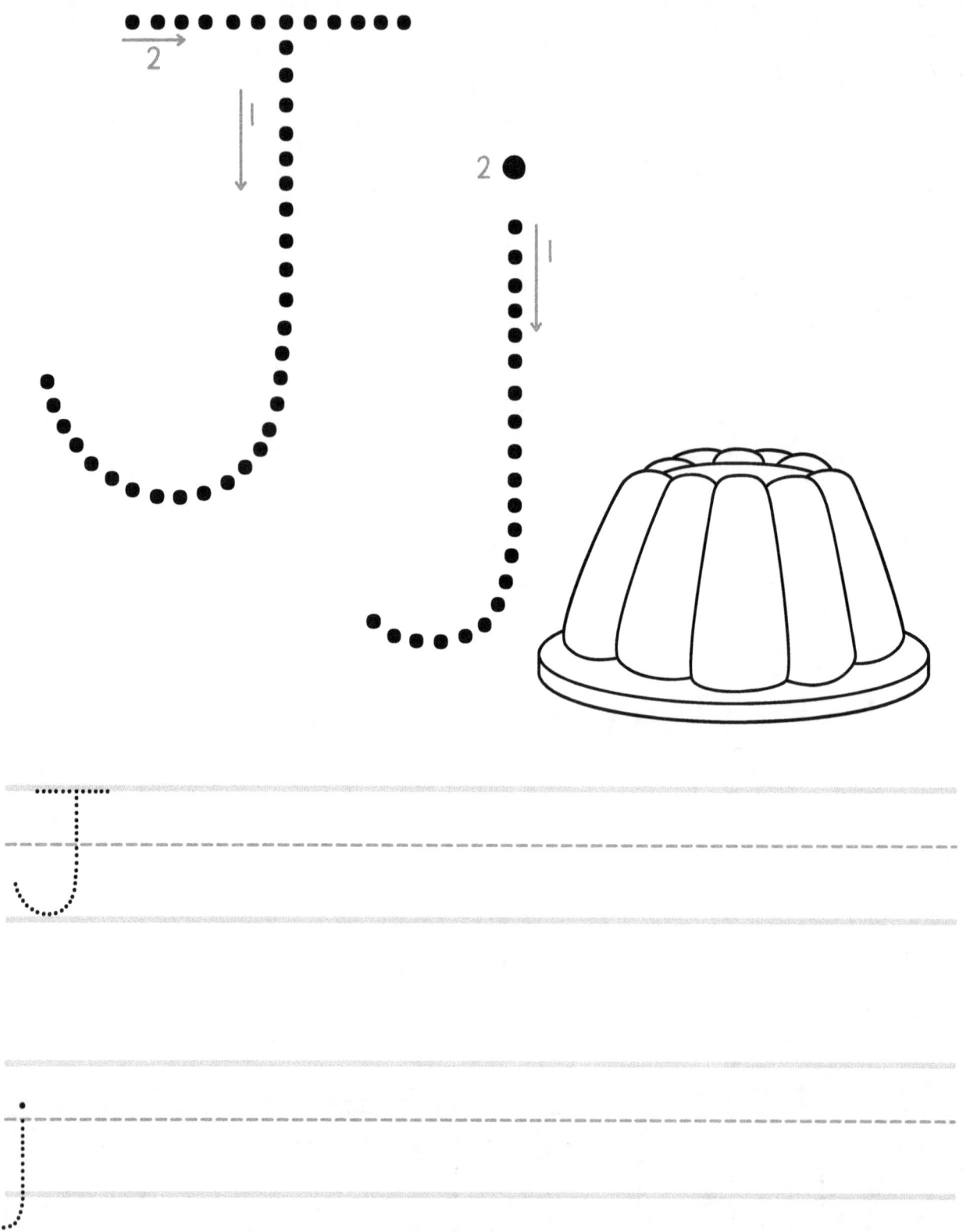

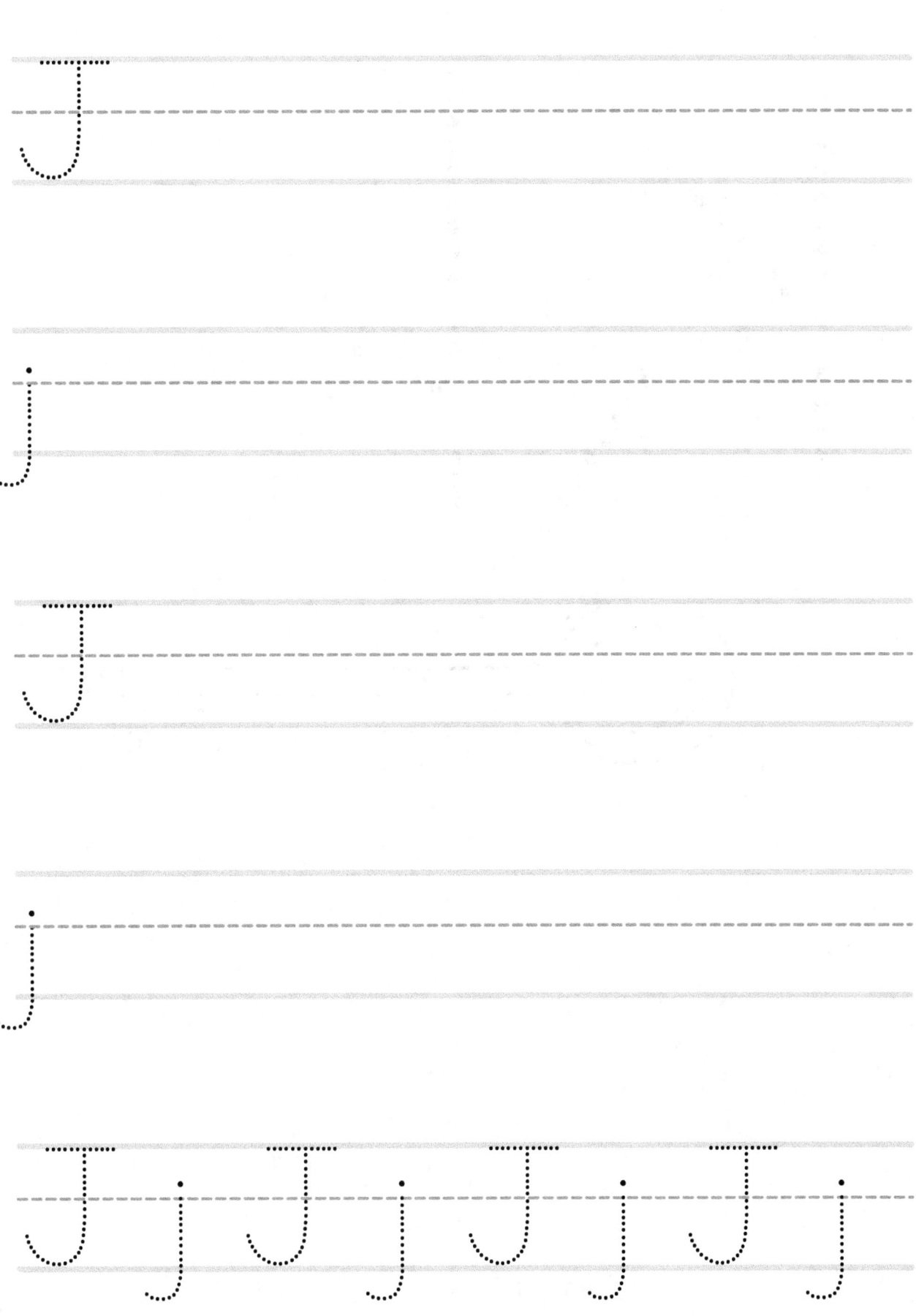

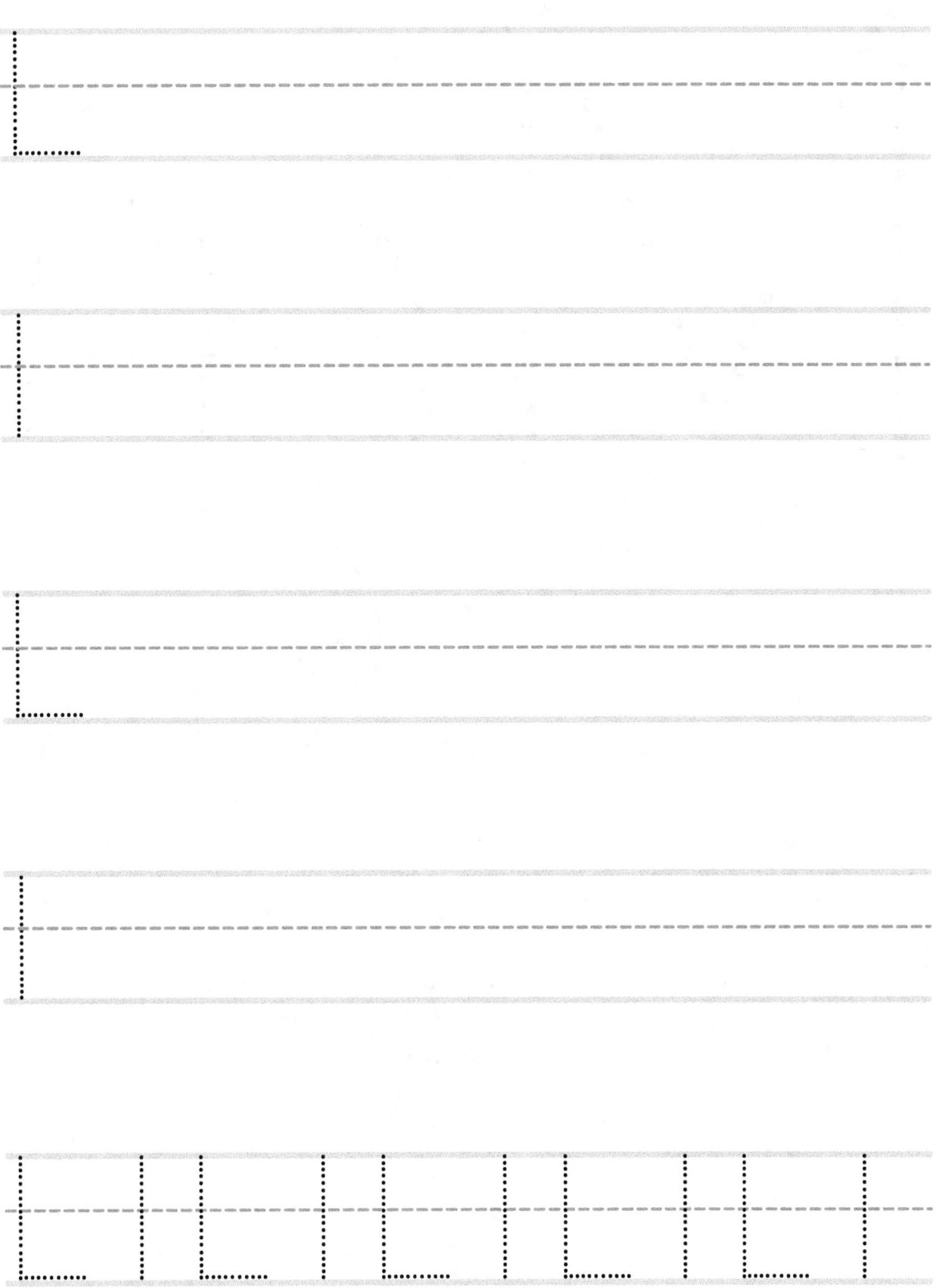

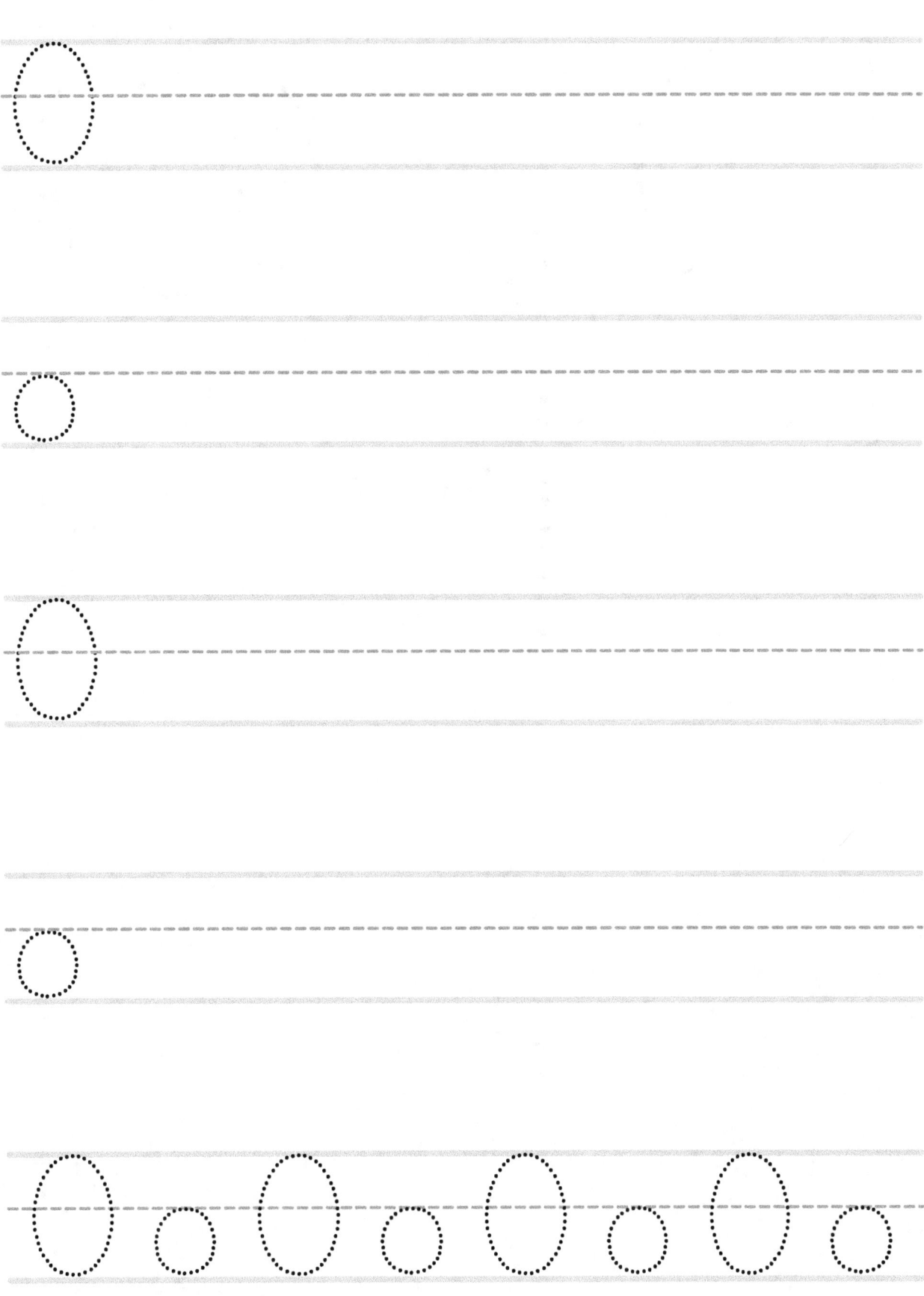

P

p

P

p

P p P p P p P p

Q

q

Q

q

Q q Q q Q q Q q

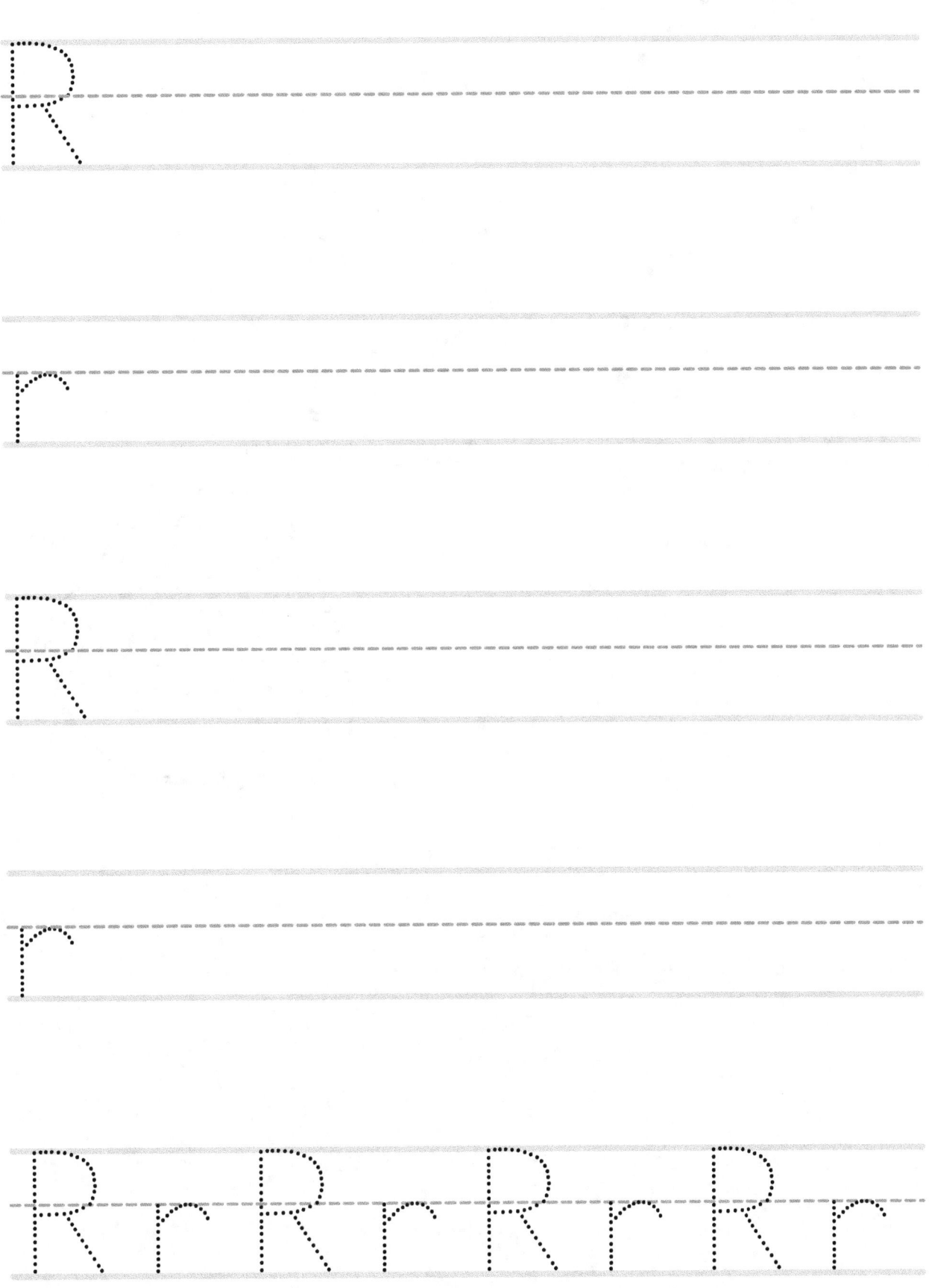

S

S

S

S

S s S s S s S s S s S s S s S

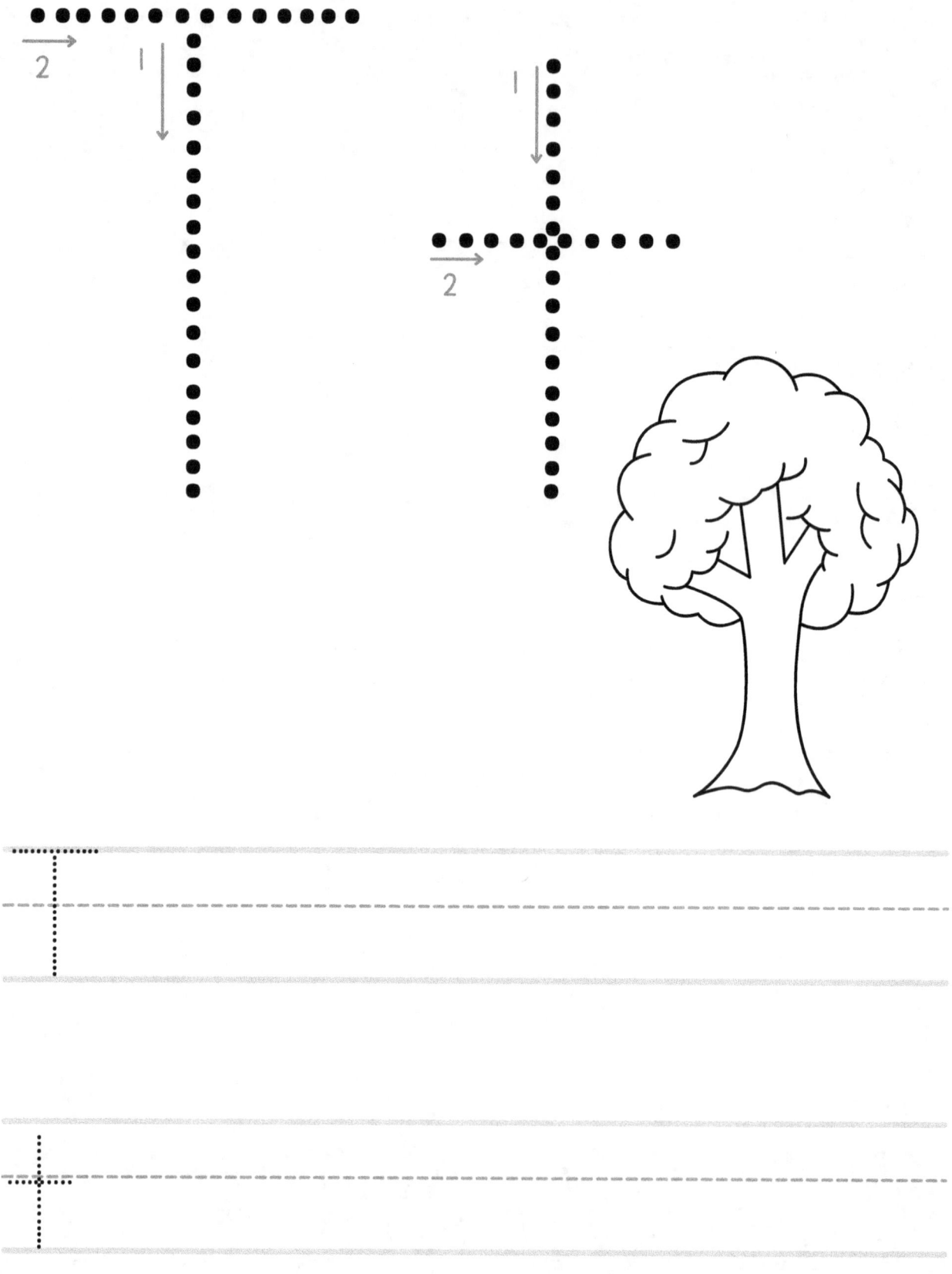

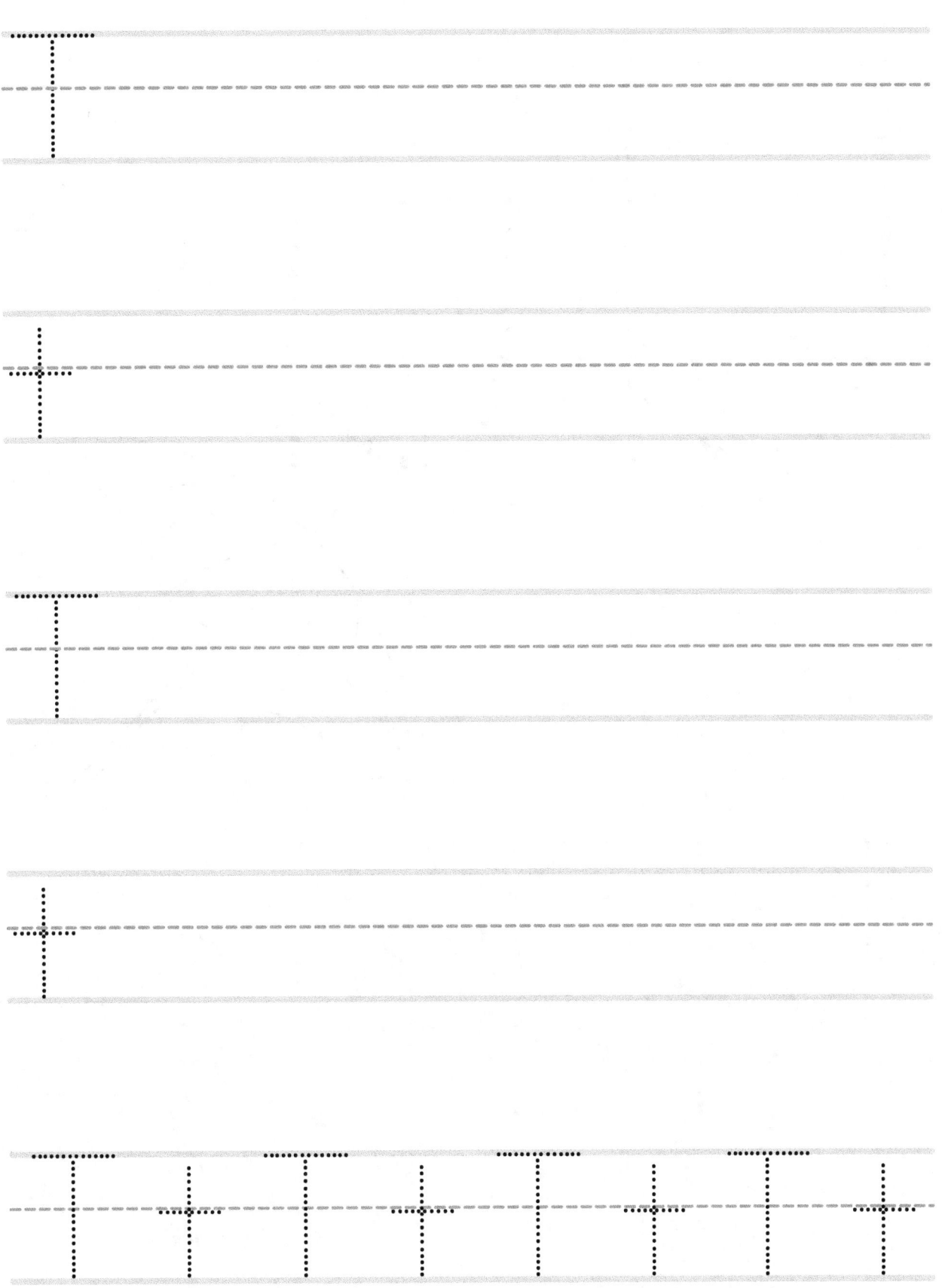

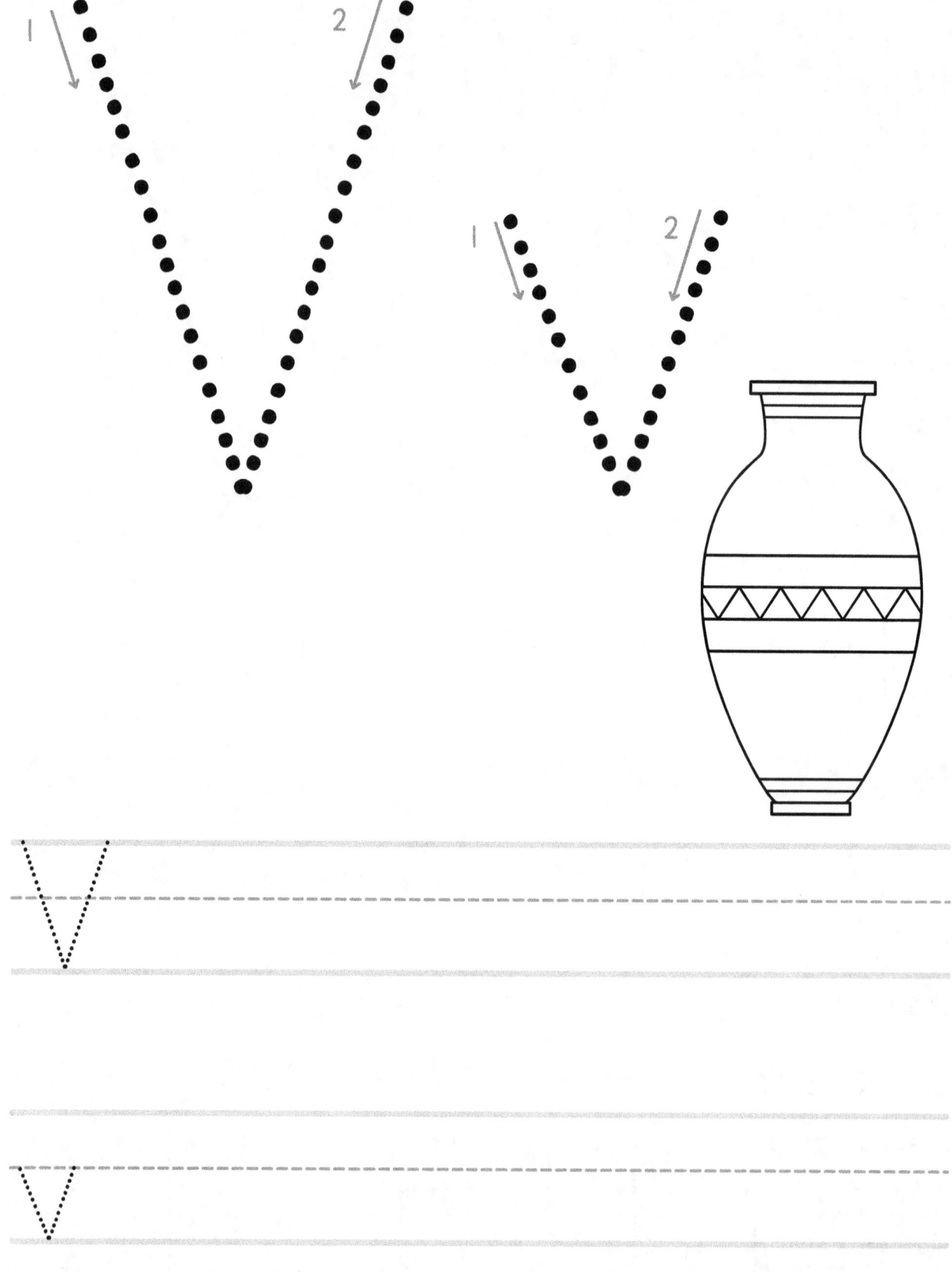

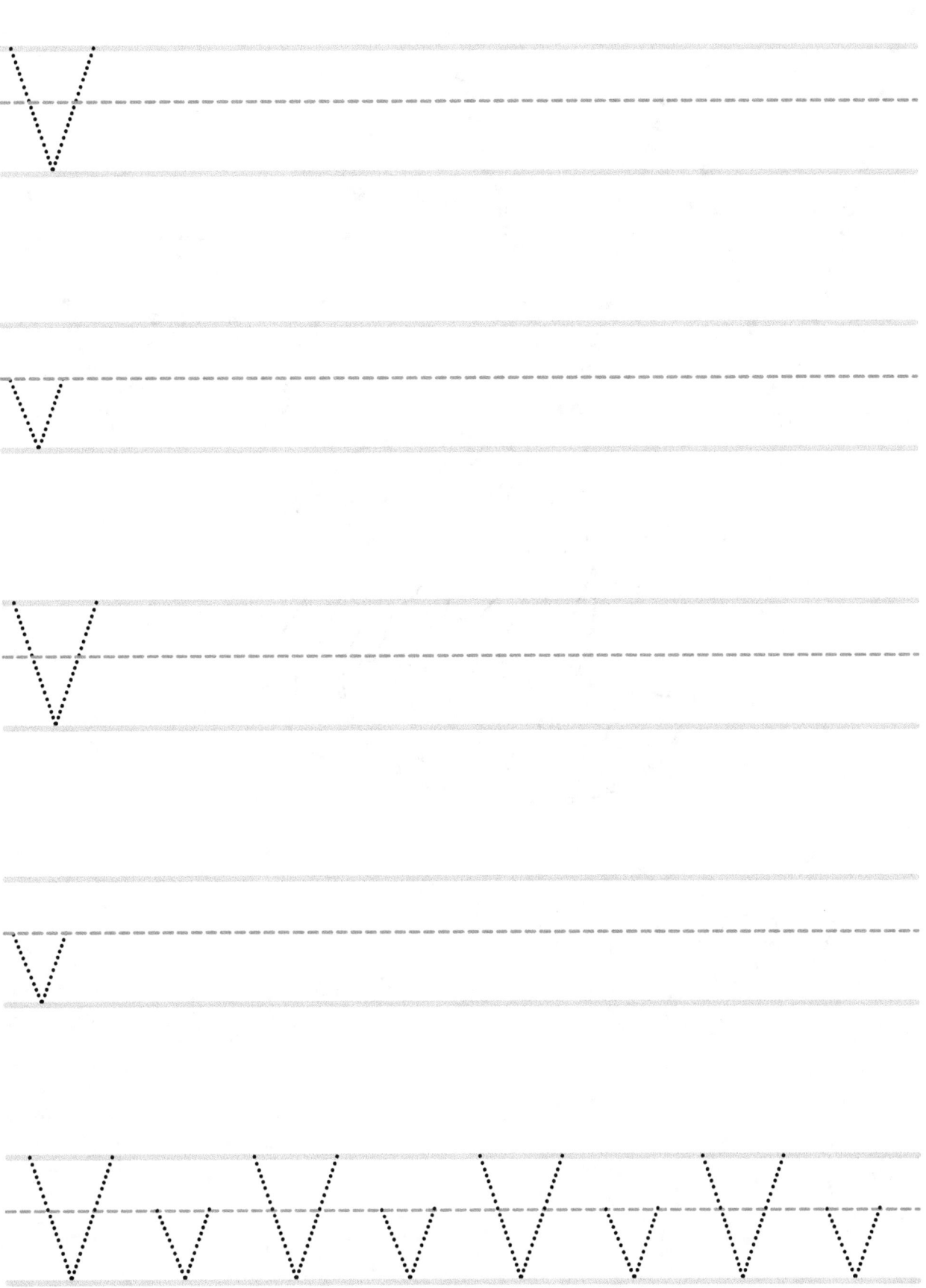

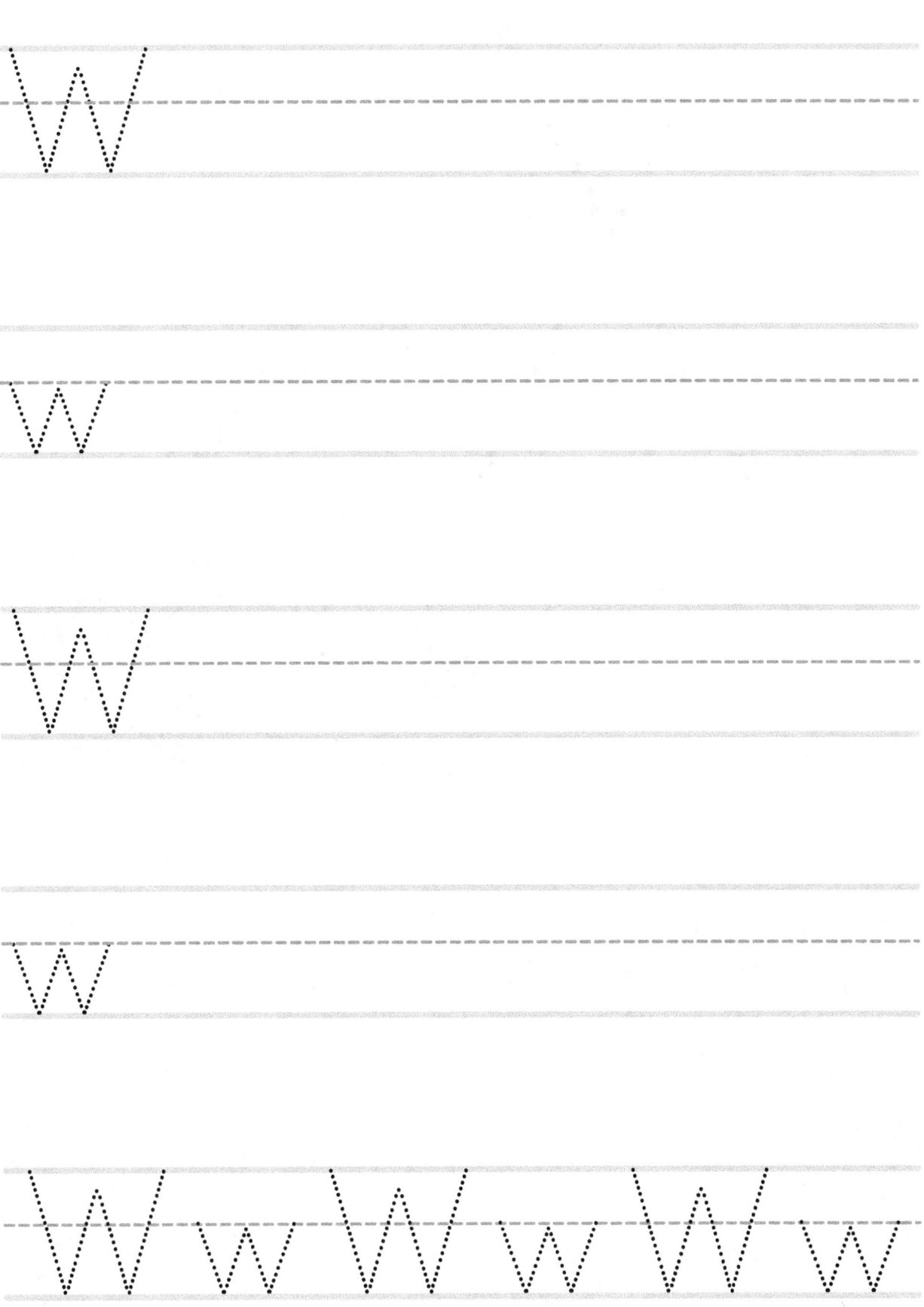

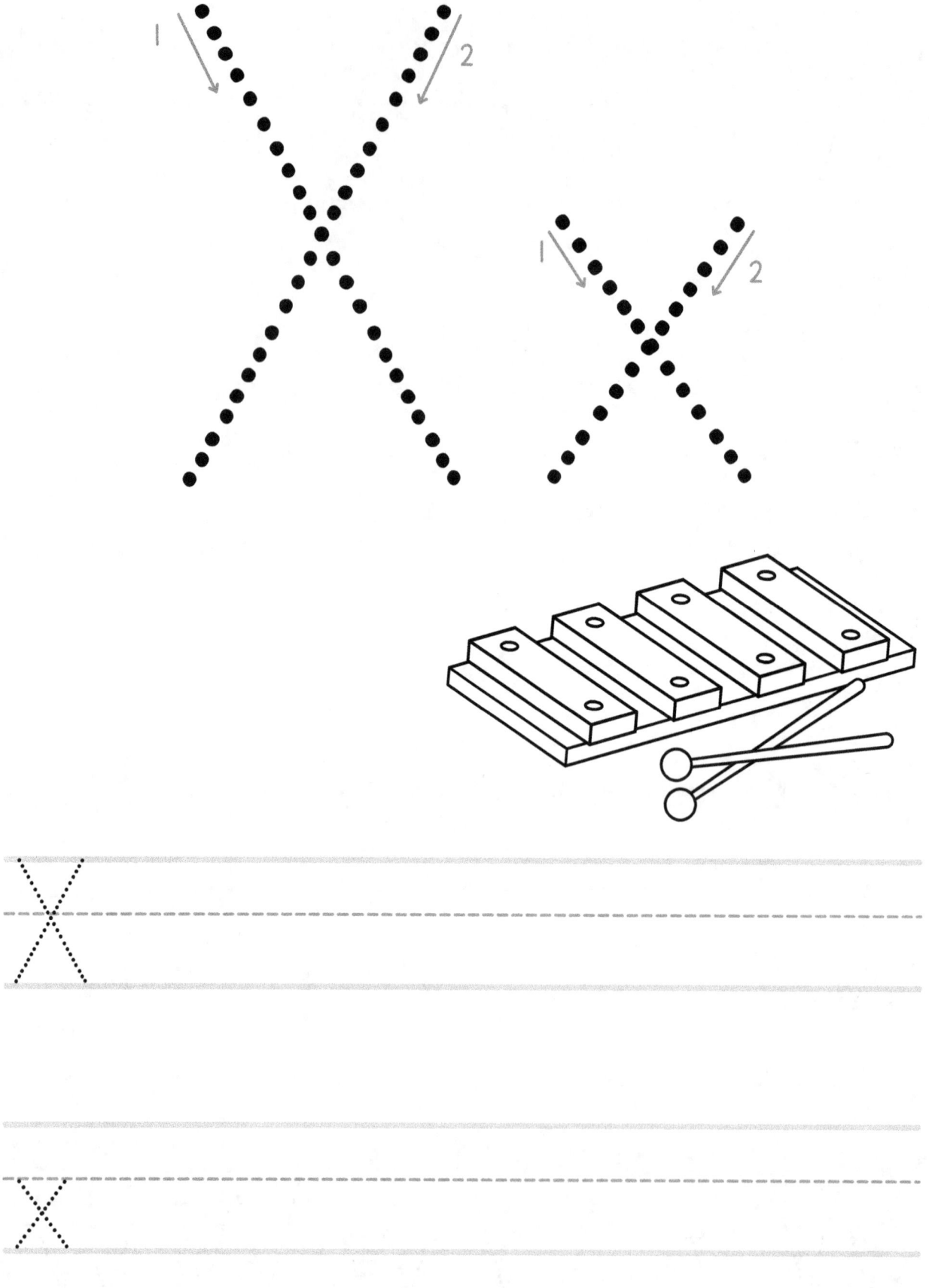

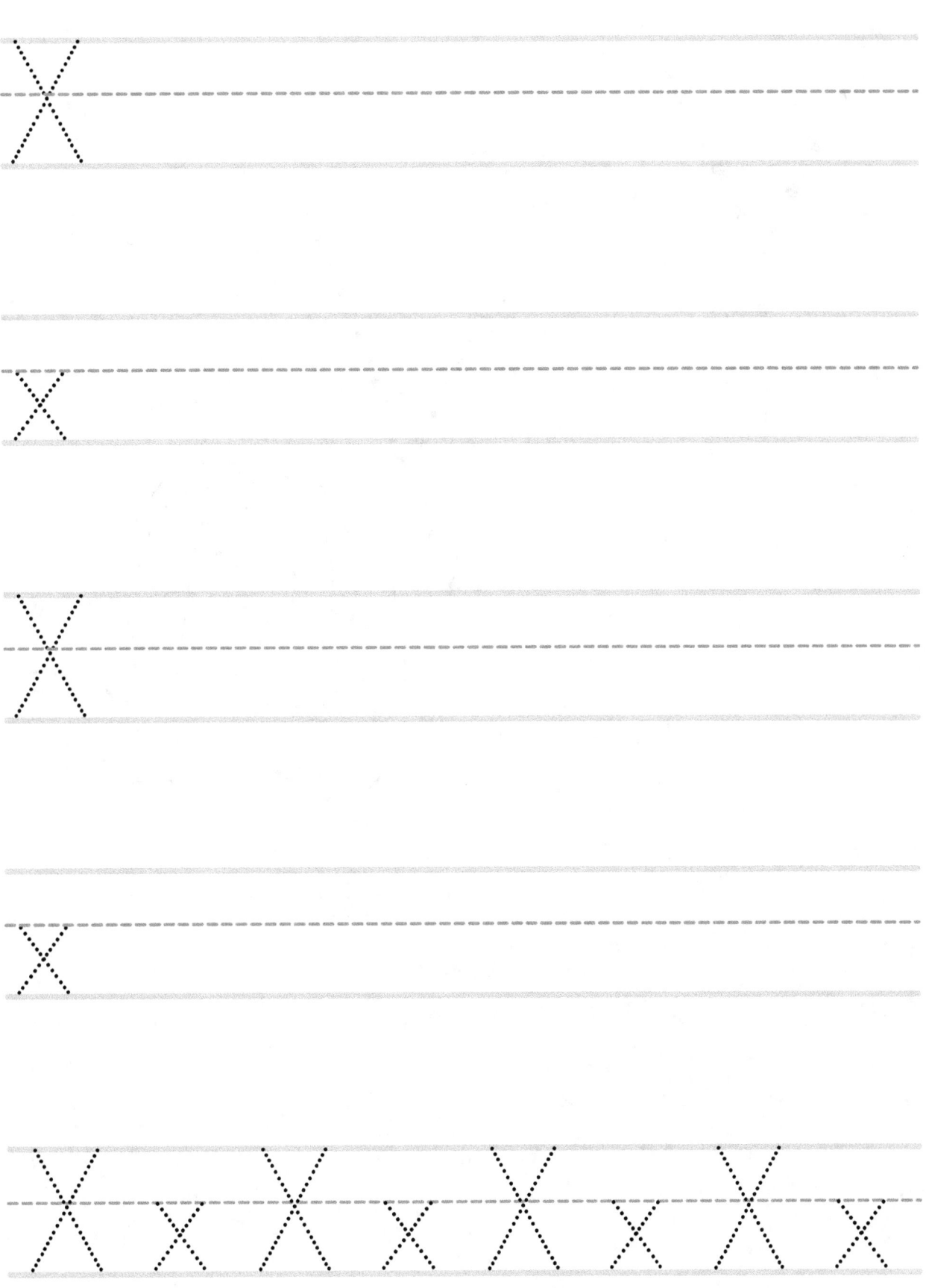

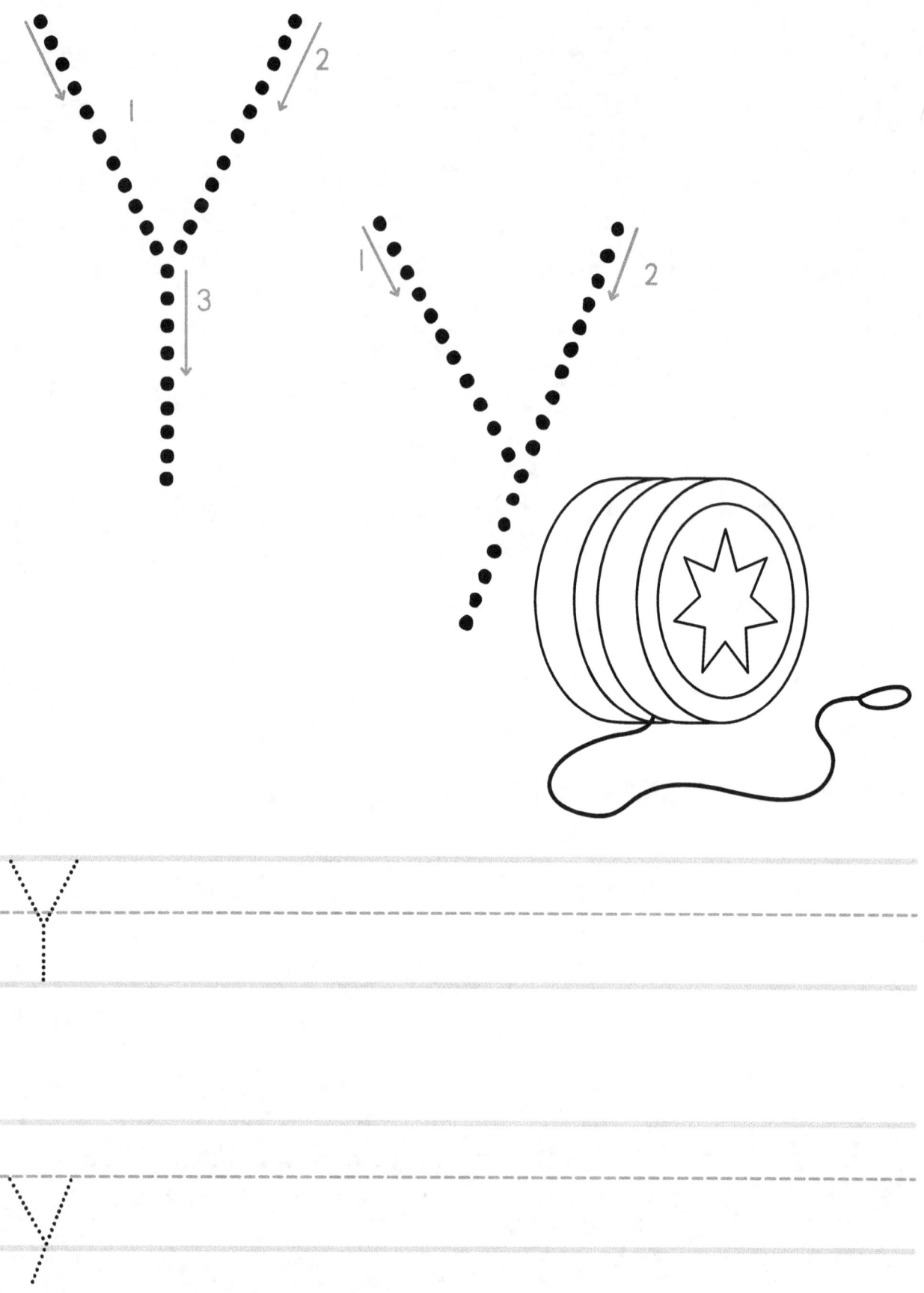

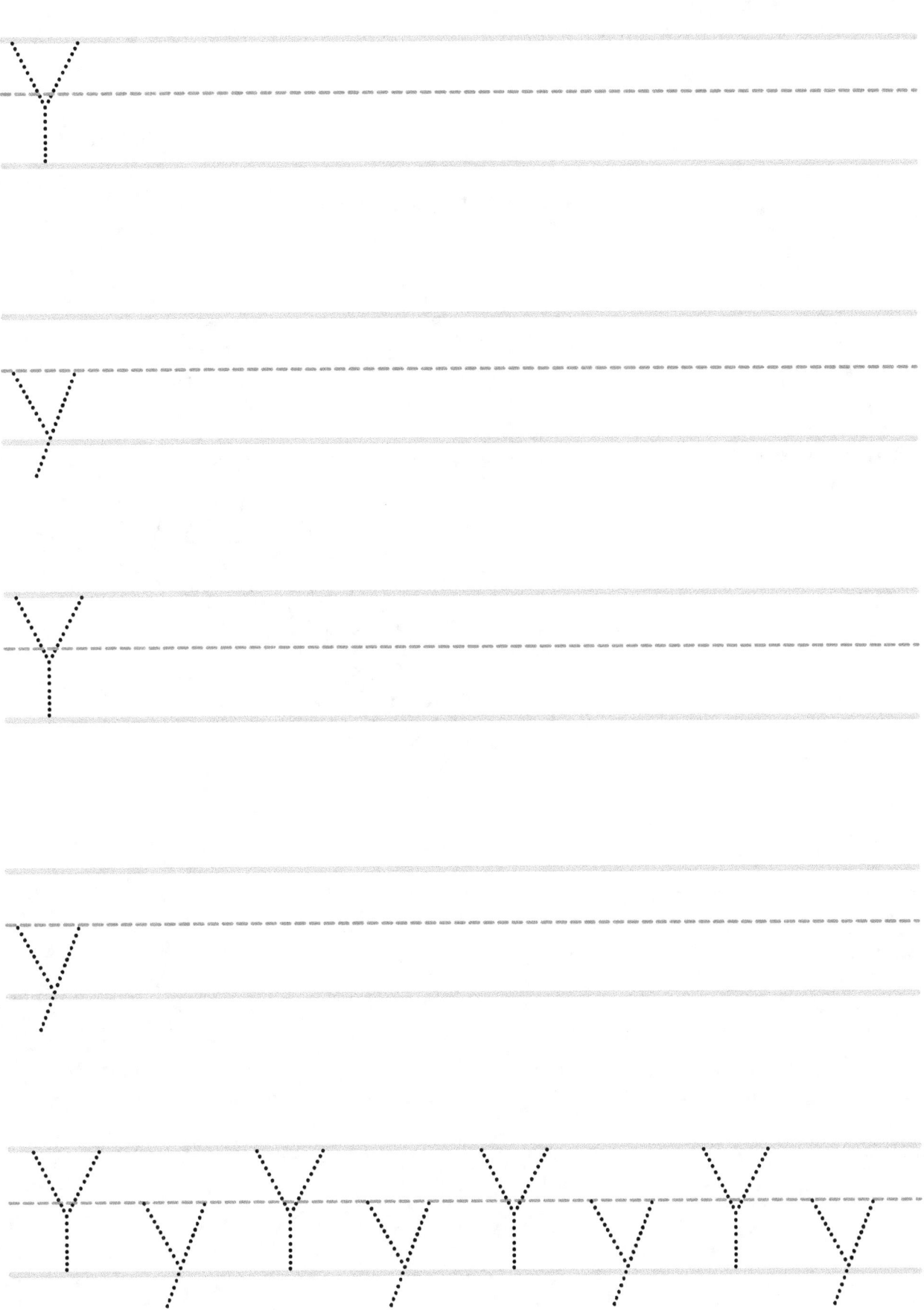

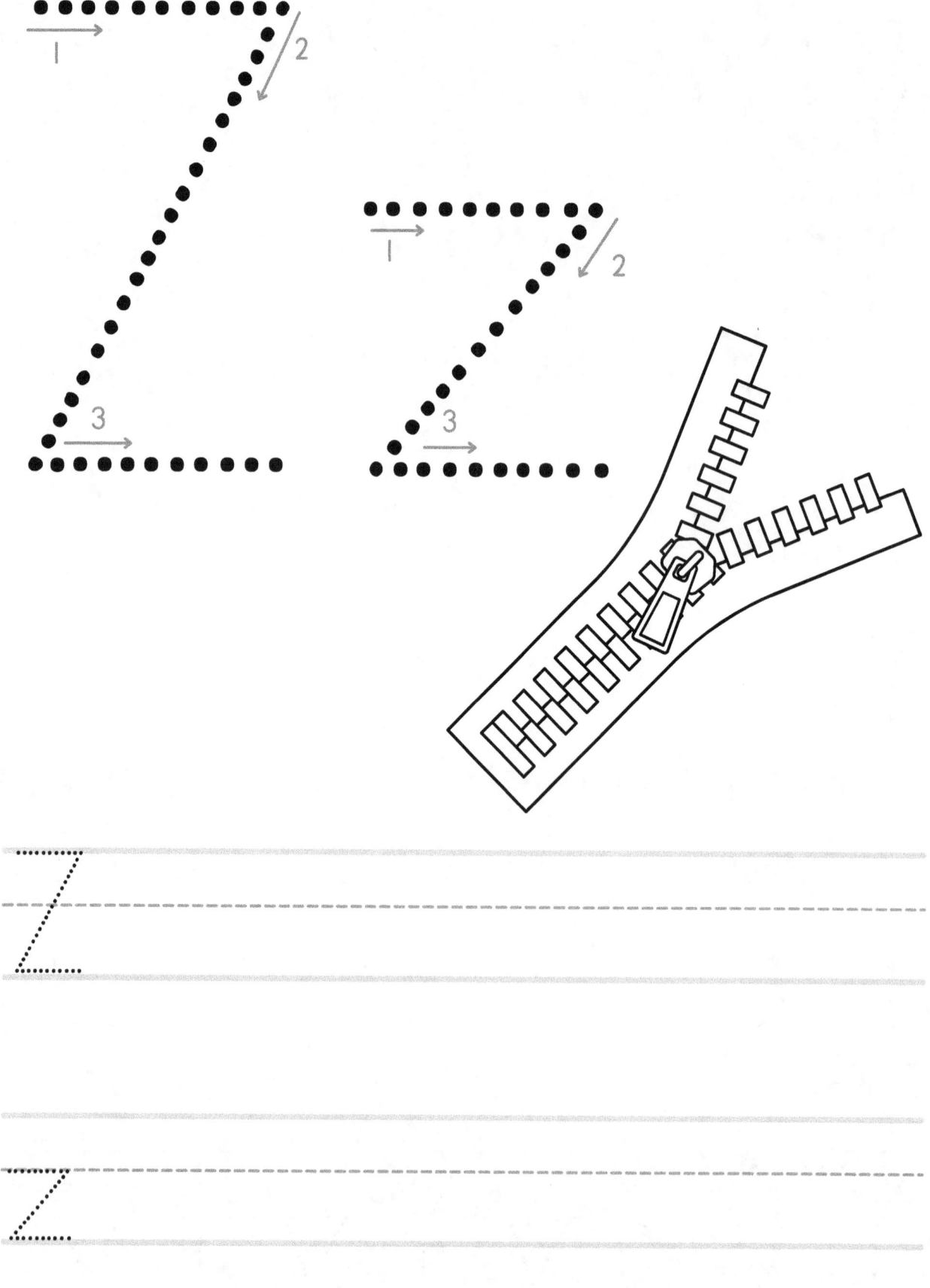

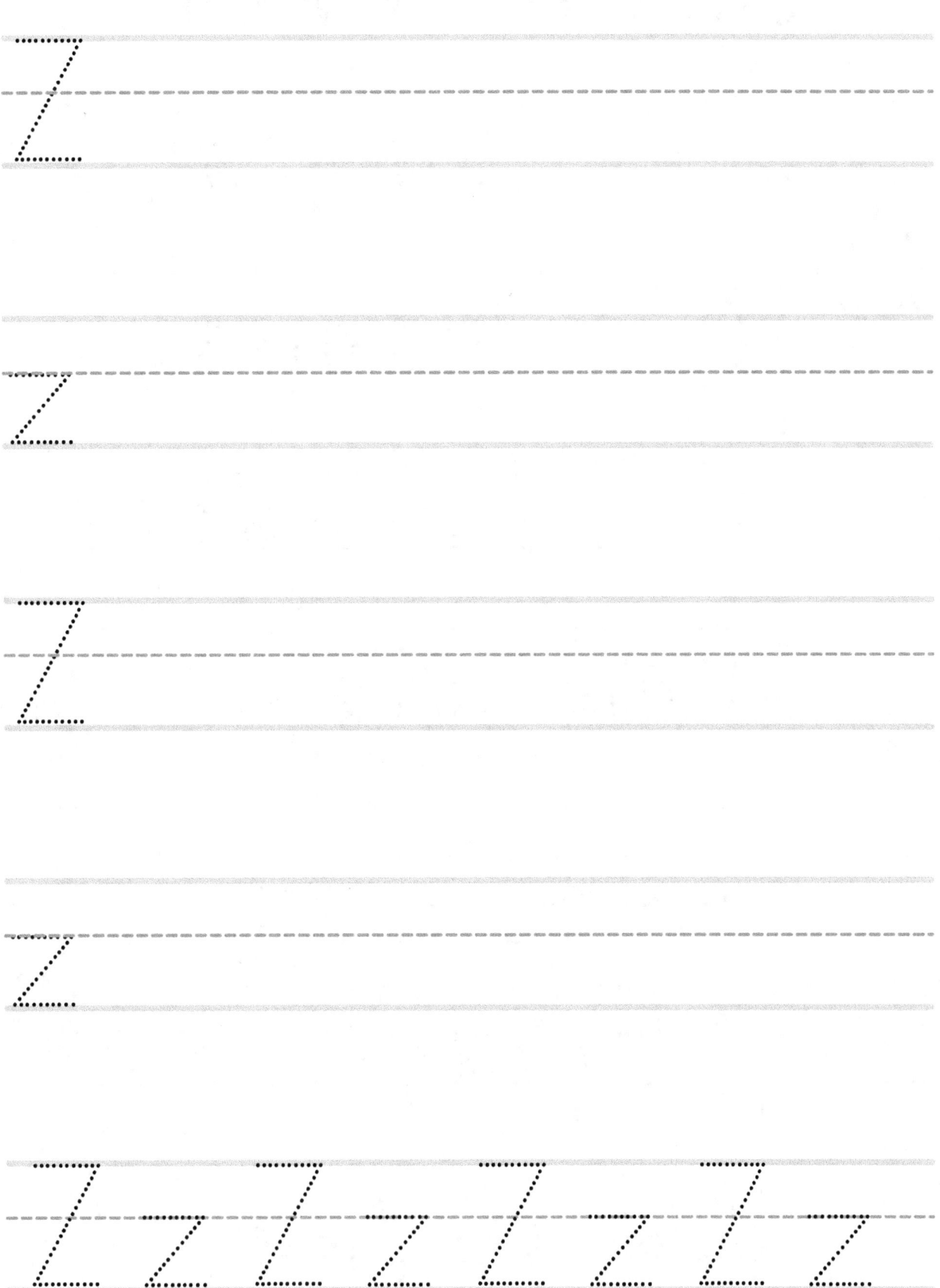

DAYS OF THE WEEK

A a

A A

a a

Anna is an amazing ant.

B b

B B

b b

Look at the busy bee.

C c

C C

c c

Carl is a colourful cow.

D d

D D

d d

Here is a dragonfly.

E e

E E

e e

Here is an elephant.

F f

F F

f f

This frog is funny.

Gg

G G

g g

The gorilla likes grapes.

H h

H   H

h   h

Henry hippo is huge.

Ii

I i

i i

Izzy iguana eats insects.

J j

J J

j j

I see a joyful jellyfish.

K k

K K

k k

Kevin the koala is kind.

L l

L L

l l

Leon the lion loves lollies.

M m

M M

m m

Mel is a cheeky monkey.

Nn

N N

n n

Newts play at night.

O o

O O

o o

Oscar is a brown otter.

P p

P P

p P

Pearl is a pretty panda.

Qq

Q Q

q q

Quokkas are quiet.

R r

R R

r r

The rooster rocks on!

S s

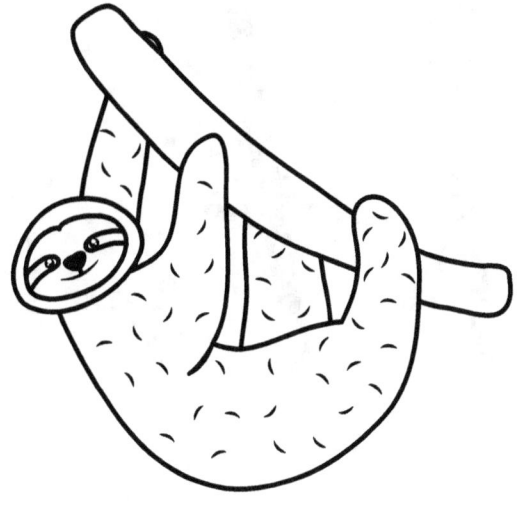

S S

s s

Sally sloth sleeps a lot.

T t

T T

t t

Terry is a tired turtle.

Uu

U u

u u

Unicorns are unique.

V v

V v

v v

Vultures are very big!

W W

w w

Whales swim in water.

 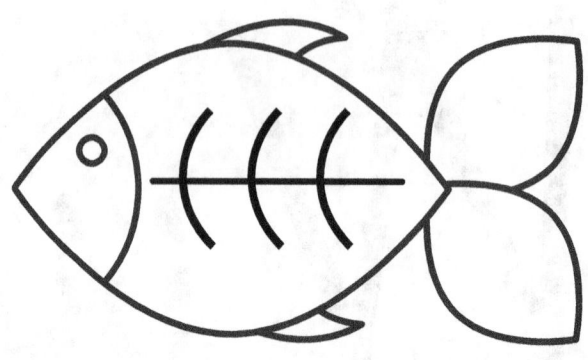

X X

x x

This is an x-ray fish.

Yy

y y

y y

The yak is funny.

Zz

Z Z

z z

Zoe the zebra zig zags.

MONTHS OF THE YEAR

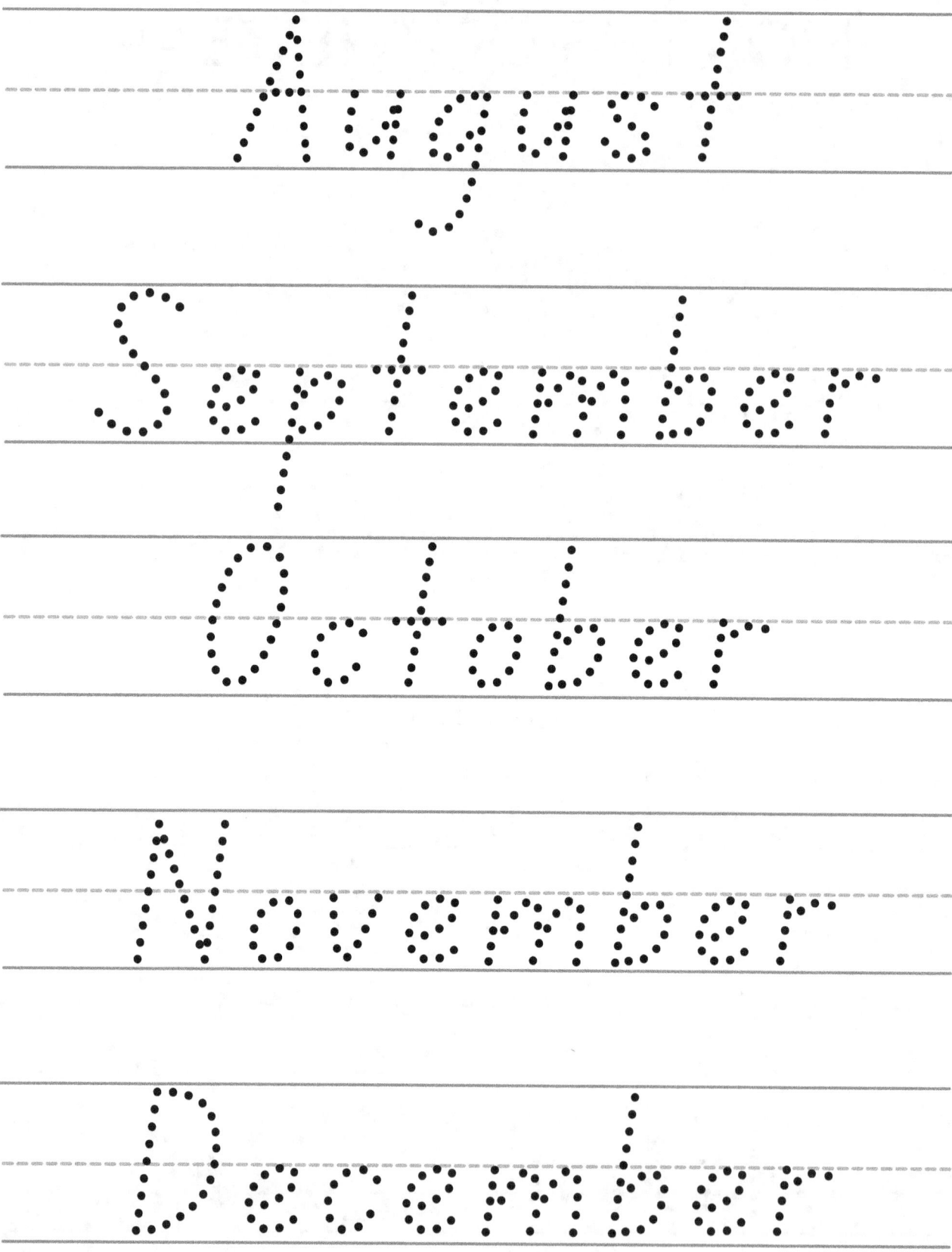

FROM ZERO TO TEN

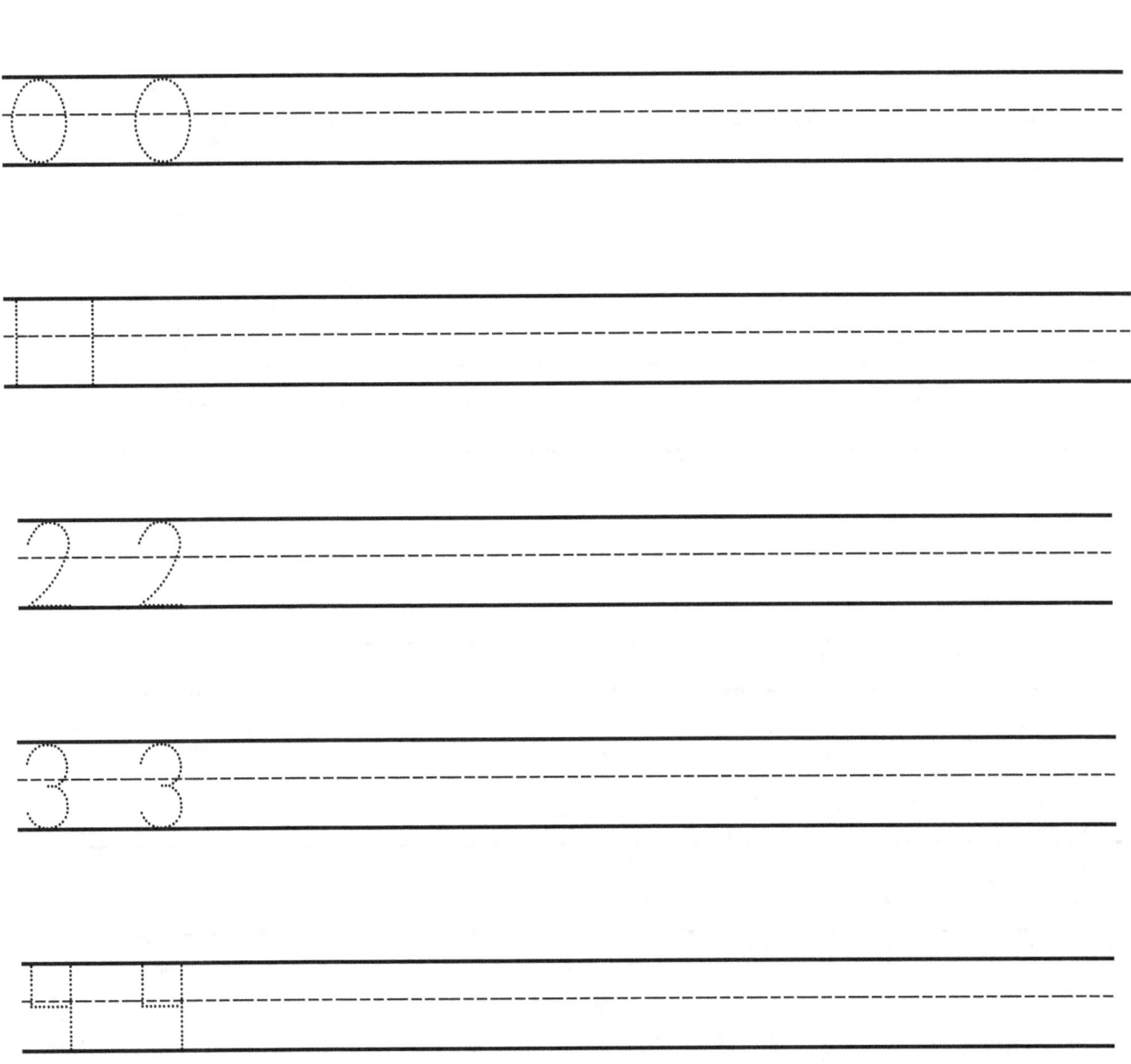

5 5

6 6

7 7

8 8

9 9

10 10

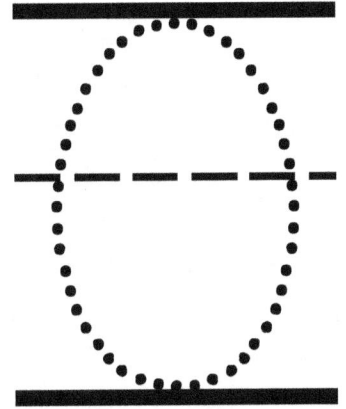

zero

I one

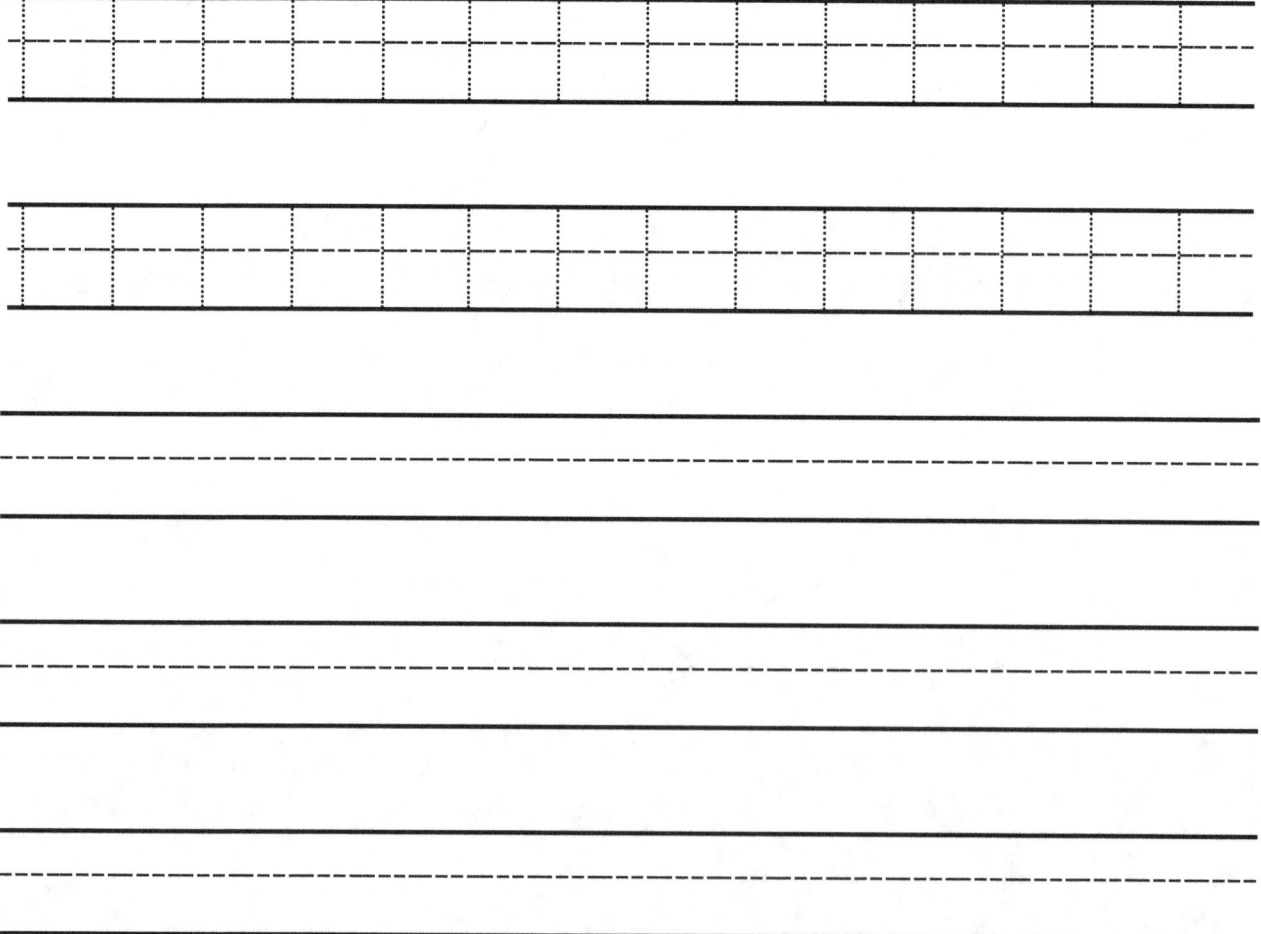

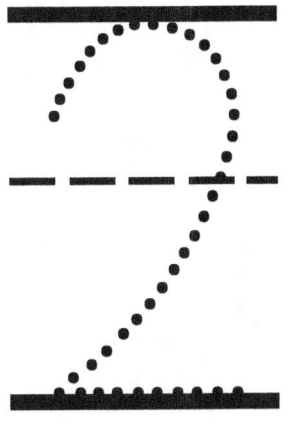

two

2 2 2 2 2 2 2 2 2 2

2 2 2 2 2 2 2 2 2 2

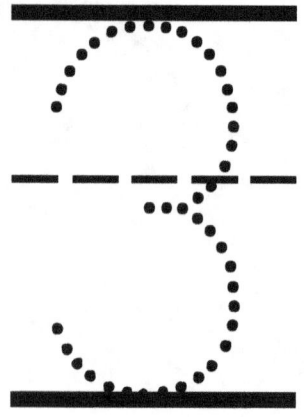

three

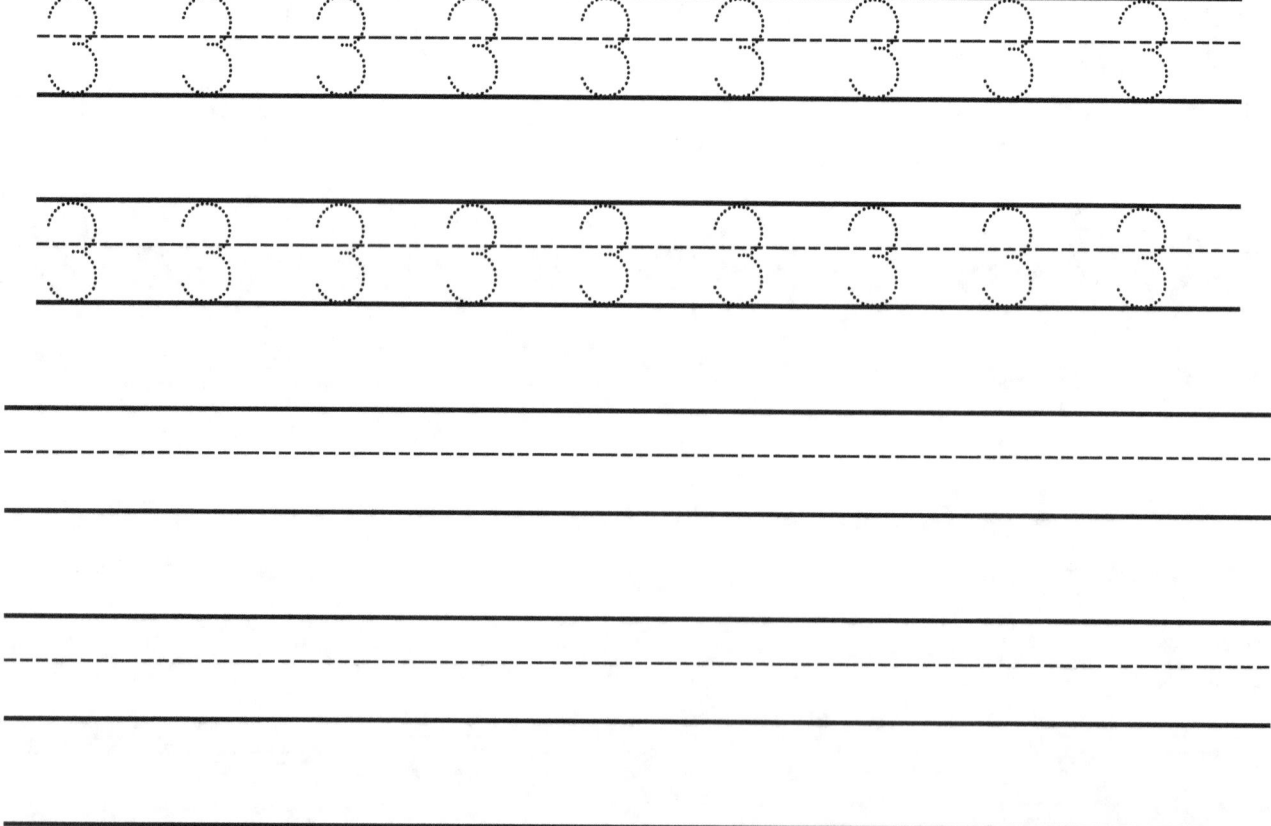

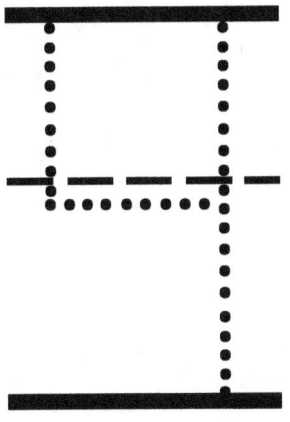

four

5

five

5 5 5 5 5 5 5 5 5 5

5 5 5 5 5 5 5 5 5 5

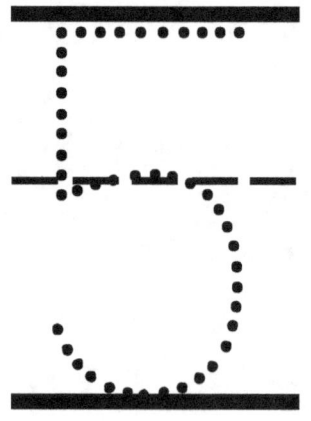

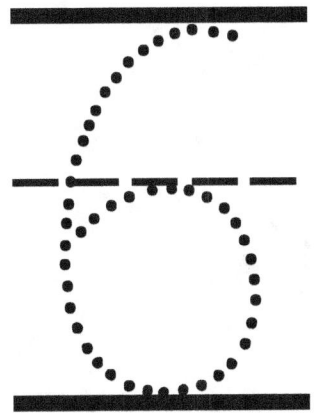

six

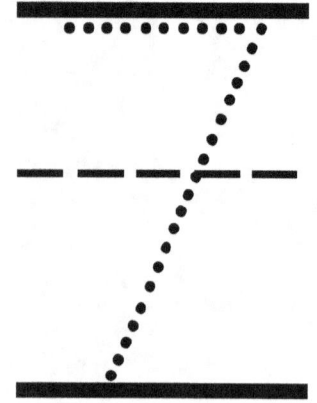

seven

8

eight

8 8 8 8 8 8 8 8 8 8

8 8 8 8 8 8 8 8 8 8

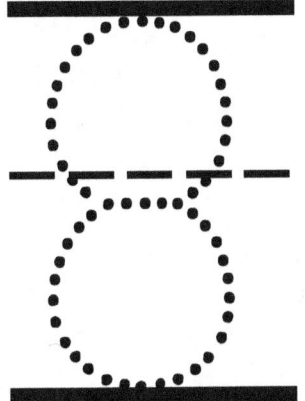

9

nine

9 9 9 9 9 9 9 9 9 9

9 9 9 9 9 9 9 9 9 9

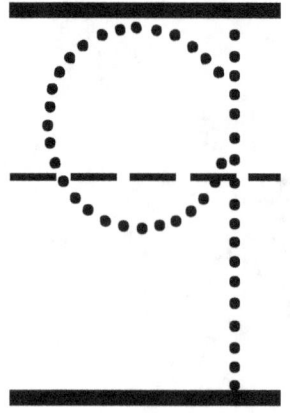

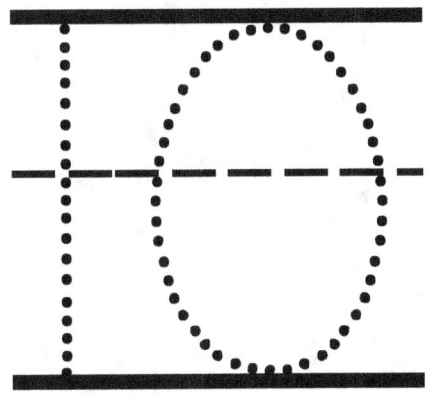

ten

10 10 10 10 10 10 10

10 10 10 10 10 10 10

THANK YOU FOR
USING THIS BOOK

www.ingramcontent.com/pod-product-compliance
Lightning Source LLC
Chambersburg PA
CBHW081722120626
46550CB00010B/3204